ELEGANTLY SIMPLE SOLUTIONS TO COMPLEX PEOPLE PROBLEMS

JAEMIN FRAZER

ELEGANTLY SIMPLE SOLUTIONS TO COMPLEX PEOPLE PROBLEMS
2018 © by Jaemin Frazer.
All rights reserved. Printed in Australia.

No part of this book may be used or reproduced in any manner whatsoever without written permission except in the case of brief quotation embodied in critical articles and reviews.

For information contact the author at *www.jaeminfrazer.com*

THIRD EDITION

Cover design by Nathan Griffith, Envoke (www.envokecreative.com)

National Library of Australia Cataloguing-in-Publication entry:

Frazer, Jaemin, author.
   Elegantly simple solutions to complex people problems / Jaemin Frazer.

ISBN: 9780994441706 (paperback)
Self-actualization (Psychology)
   Personal coaching.
   Performance.
   Success.
158.1

ACKNOWLEDGEMENTS

To my wife. You have loved me through the process of becoming the kind of man who could contribute meaningfully in the world. This book is the fruit of that love. Thank you.

CONTENTS

Acknowledgements	iii
Preface	1
PART I - THE COACHING FRAME	
Introduction	11
Chapter 1: The Judgment Free Space	15
Chapter 2: Being Outcomes Focused	25
Chapter 3: Having Increased Awareness	35
Chapter 4: People Work Perfectly	59
Chapter 5: Everything Can Be Reframed	71
Chapter 6: State is King	83
PART II - A MODEL FOR CHANGE	
Introduction	107
Chapter 7: Hopelessness	109
Chapter 8: The Illusion of No Choice	115
Chapter 9: Embracing 100% Choice	119
Chapter 10: Hope	137
Chapter 11: Helplessness	141
Chapter 12: Giving Your Power Away	145
Chapter 13: Taking 100% Responsibility	149
Chapter 14: Personal Power	153
Chapter 15: Hurtfulness	159
Chapter 16: Neediness	165
Chapter 17: 100% Ownership	177
Chapter 18: Humour	191
Wrapping it All Up	197
Endnotes	199

PREFACE

"Things should be made as simple as possible and no simpler."
—**Albert Einstein**

While away on a three day book writing retreat on the south coast of NSW, I was sitting overlooking the beach when an elderly man stopped and struck up a conversation with me about the beautiful view. I asked him a bit about himself and how long he'd lived there. We had an interesting conversation that ended abruptly when I told him I was writing a personal development book. "Oh forget that," he said and he walked off!

What a crazy idea, to develop yourself! Earn money, work 10 hours a day for 40 years and then retire. Get married, have kids then have grandkids. Buy a car, go on holidays, watch movies, drink beer or talk to your neighbours about the weather, but whatever you do, don't develop your own life. Do not grow your character and deal with your doubts, fears and insecurities. What a crazy waste of time right?

I'm not sure if you've noticed, but the road less travelled[1] is in no danger of being trampled and overrun by the masses. Most people will never invest in personal development work and really achieve what they are capable of.

Henry David Thoreau famously said "The mass of men will lead lives of quiet desperation[2]." They will remain in situations and environments that they don't like but feel powerless to change. They will continue to follow the crowd and operate at a level far beneath their best. They will choose safety and survival over growth and change and continue to be severely limited by doubt, fear and insecurity their whole lives.

I'm convinced that to succeed in life is actually quite easy, because most people never will. You only have to do a few key things semi-consistently and it quickly separates you from the crowd. Every day we have access to everything that we need to live well, but most people will choose to ignore it and keep doing what they've always done.

I'm guessing by the fact that you picked this book up in the first place, you are not that guy at the beach. Let me tell you, that makes you a very rare individual in the history of the world. May you find what you are looking for and become great at being you.

Complicated and Unique Problems

So often we experience our problems as being extremely complicated and totally unique. To be fair, that is exactly how it seems at the time. It's very common to find ourselves in messy situations, coping with relational obligations or entangled in a web of constant trouble. At such times, it's very easy to imagine that no one else has experienced the same challenges, and that we are all alone trying to find a way out. It can be astounding to discover that while the solution may not be easy, it is definitely not complicated. Often people confuse simple with easy. Instead, the path to success is always simple and hard.

What's more, we are not as isolated and our challenges are not as unique as they might seem. Although the specifics may vary from person to person, we all go through the same story in some way, battling exactly the same kinds of doubts, fears and insecurities. So it turns out, our problems are actually neither complicated nor unique. The beautiful thing is that there is a clear framework you can use to find your way out of the mess and move beyond simply surviving to truly flourishing as the person you were created to be.

My greatest passion is personal development. I have discovered some of the very best tools for transformational change through my journey into coaching. I love the quality of the coaching space to open the doors to freedom and life. Finding freedom isn't common, but it is possible. Change, growth and even personal congruence are available to each of us, although only very few will ever taste the joy of a life well lived.

Madness

Eckhart Tolle[3] says that if you condensed the history of mankind down into the life of a single human being, that person would be undeniably labelled as a violent, psychopathic, madman. Madness seems to be the only word that does justice to our predicament.

If you were to float into space and simply observe the way we do life on earth, you would see inherently good, valuable and creative people who consistently make daily decisions to hurt themselves, others and the planet. It is madness. That is the only way it can be described.

One of the most extraordinary things in the universe is our ability to survive and suffer in deeply dysfunctional situations. People may truly hate their circumstances and complain about how terrible they are, but then still get up each new day and do it all over again without making any changes. It really is remarkable!

Most people will continue to survive in dysfunction, right up to the point of madness. It's the human condition. So many good people, despite their best efforts, go through life hurting themselves and others.

All the world's major religions agree that the normal way of living for human beings is deeply dysfunctional to the point of madness. The Buddhist way of understanding it is called dukka—suffering, unsatisfactoriness or just plain misery. In the Hindu teachings, it is called maya—the veil of delusion. The Christians call it sin. The word sin means to miss the mark, which is really interesting because it means to suffer from sin (madness) is that we miss the point of what it means to be human in the first place.

Each religion also agrees that there is a way out of the madness through a radical transformation of human consciousness. In Hindu teachings it is called enlightenment. In Buddhism it is the end of suffering and in the teachings of Jesus it is called salvation and in[4], yet paradoxically it is not through religion as such that one becomes free.

The essence of Jesus' message, for example, is all about coming home and finding yourself as a fully formed human being, yet often people become Christian only by making a mental assent to accept the deity of Jesus without ever actually dealing with the madness.

Religious systems often end up being a place of self-righteousness and judgment, which ironically causes religious people to propagate madness in the world!

The good news is that there are ways out of the madness for those who are ready to find and themselves and break free.

Framing

A stark white page appears quite different with a black frame than it does with a pink one; it is as though the shade of white changes before your very eyes simply by changing the frame! Changing the frame also changes your experience of what's inside the frame. The same is true in life. The frame we bring to each situation (and through which we understand what is happening to us) shapes our experience of that situation. The frame consists of our culture, beliefs, values and experiences, each of which colour how we interpret every moment of our lives. Two people can be in the same situation yet because of their different cultures, beliefs or values, they will each experience their reality very differently. This is all due to the power of the frame.

Every conversation we have is experienced through a frame. This allows us to make sense of what we are hearing and informs us about what we should expect from the words being exchanged. It is impossible to have a frame free conversation, because we are sense-making creatures. Even if the frame has not been agreed on or made explicit, subconsciously we always assume a frame based on past experience, generalisations and default beliefs.

Types of frames

The frame we bring to a conversation with a friend is very different to the one we use as parent, child, business partner, employee, boss, spouse, expert, coach, mentor, stranger, customer, teacher or student. Take for example the words 'can you clean up that mess?' These are totally appropriate when coming from your spouse, parent or boss but can be totally offensive when spoken by a friend, stranger or employee. The exact same conversation in a different context or a different frame will produce a completely different result. Getting the framing wrong can create massive relational problems. Saying the right words under the wrong frame will get you into trouble every time.

Framing conversations is particularly critical when we have multiple frames available with the same person. For example, you and another person might be related, share the same work environment and also be part of a local sporting club i.e. brother, employee and teammate. If you are not conscious of which frame you're under at what time, you can easily cause relationship pain without intending to.

Before we go any further, let me show you how I've arranged this book. It is split into two sections.

Part 1 – The Coaching Frame

Coaching has a frame too. It doesn't supersede other frames. All the other relationship frames are just as necessary and important in their place, but if you're looking for leverage for change, it is the only appropriate frame to use.

Life coaching is cheeky. It steals all the best tools from counselling, psychology and human behavioural science and frames them extraordinarily well. It is my experience that the right frame, plus the best tools delivers the most powerful leverage for change available.

If you are looking for elegantly simple solutions to your complicated problems, and a way out of the madness, then I suggest you see this conversation we are having right now through the coaching frame. If you are looking for sympathy or you are not willing to accept your part in the mess in your life, then the coaching frame will only cause you grief. (Don't say I didn't warn you!)

Part 2 – A Model for Change

In the second part I'll share with you the 'Hope, Power, Humour' model for change. This model consistently delivers elegantly simple solutions for complicated people problems when accessed through the lens of the coaching frame.

I challenge you to commit to reading the whole book and understanding the complete system so you don't get vaccinated. Too many people 'dabble' and 'try', convincing themselves that the reason they don't get the results they are looking for is because the tools they use are faulty or inadequate. Let me assure you that there is nothing wrong with these tools or the model I am proposing. What you are about to read has been tried and tested. If you only half use it or use it halfheartedly, it will not work. If you use this framework as presented, not only will it work, but it will yield amazing results.

Part One

THE COACHING FRAME

INTRODUCTION

Your experience of what you see is totally coloured by the lens you look through. In this section we will explore the coaching frame. Viewing the world through this frame will provide you with a new way of seeing things and give you access to change in a way you have likely not experienced before.

There are six key pieces of the coaching frame that make it so effective. Each of these pieces can seem quite counter-intuitive and they are certainly counter-cultural, yet I guarantee that together they create a powerful frame that you'll find incredibly useful for improving the quality and consistency of the results you are getting. In fact I'd go as far as to say the coaching frame will help you to see and experience just how real, simple and tangible change can be and that, somewhat surprisingly, change can be yours as soon as you want it.

In the following chapters I will cover each piece of the frame in detail. I suggest you revisit these chapters frequently until you have a thorough understanding of the coaching frame so it becomes your lens of choice when you are looking for change. That way you can use it with volition and flexibility to suit your purpose and desired outcomes.

Understanding each of these elements and how they work together will enable you to access the full transformational power of the model for change that will follow.

It is my hope that once you understand the coaching frame, you will choose to adopt it as the frame through which you will experience the conversations we have throughout the remainder of this book

Chapter One

THE JUDGMENT FREE SPACE

Wanting people to change is by far the least effective way of motivating them to do so.

On a recent flight, I was watching an American sitcom called 'Surviving Jack.' It's about a guy who retires from being a doctor in the armed forces. He swaps roles with his wife so that she can enter the work force while he stays home and takes over the major parenting duties for their teenage children. Set in the 1980's, it is a very humorous look at all the challenges faced by teenagers growing up in the real world, not to mention the struggles their parents face while trying to help them navigate these stormy seas.

I wasn't expecting it to be that interesting, but five minutes into the first episode I was hooked. I laughed and cried all the way to Brisbane, oblivious to what others might have thought. As far as I was concerned, I was the only person on the plane. I was a teenager once. I had to face all the same challenges that were being presented on the T.V. show. In some areas I did really well; in others I struggled. I made some great choices and I made some really poor ones too. I had some great days and some horrible ones (didn't we all?), yet none of the events of my teenage years changed the fact that I'm OK. I'm not a bad person. What people think of me today and the deep characteristics of who I really am were not determined by my choices or behaviour as a teenager. I not only survived those years, but I came out well.

My kids are not far off teenage years themselves. It's like they are sitting on 'free parking' on the Monopoly board game, about to roll the dice and turn the corner onto 'The Strand', 'Fleet Street' and 'Trafalgar Square'. Past that is 'Leicester', 'Coventry' and 'Piccadilly', not to mention 'Regent', 'Oxford' and 'Bond' and then finally 'Park Lane' and 'Mayfair'. All the properties are loaded with hotels, their owners licking their lips, waiting… willing the dice to roll in their favour. My kids are about to face some of the biggest challenges of their entire lives. Issues of identity, self-esteem, sexuality, peer pressure, drugs and alcohol, relationships and career path choices sit in front of them like a minefield of potential hazards.

I want my kids to be OK. More than that, I want them to make the right choices and not get hurt or sidetracked along the way. Yet as I was watching this show, blowing snot into a serviette, I was struck by the fact that I can't make them do well. I can't make their choices for them or ensure that they don't get hurt. While they are my precious children, I don't actually own them. They are their own people. I have been given the incredible privilege of being in their world, walking alongside them in this season of life. I have the opportunity to be either a help or a hindrance to them in these few years we have together.

We all want our friends and family to be happy and make great choices. It's a natural desire we have towards those we love and care about. Yet interestingly, all the wanting in the world doesn't actually produce any real change. In fact, wanting someone to change, grow or make healthy choices may in fact be the least effective way of positively influencing them to change.

Think about the conversations you've had with your parents, your kids or your friends, particularly when you suggested what should or shouldn't be happening. As the suggestion giver you feel like the advice will be useful and is coming from the right motivation. The receiver often feels like the suggestion is not really about them at all, but about what you want—and to be honest… it usually is. We want, or even need others to do and be certain things to make ourselves feel better about our own lives. Unfortunately, when we communicate this wanting to those we love, it is experienced as a judgment. It's rightly received as an imposition of our views, expectations, rules and map of reality onto the other person, and that never goes well.

Wanting someone to do something, even for all the 'right' reasons, only produces expectation, obligation, pressure and judgment. This external and temporary form of motivation does not hang around once you leave the room. Lasting motivation, by contrast, is always internally driven.

Wanting, pushing and suggesting simply doesn't produce the desired change. No matter how well intentioned you are, it really is a form of judgment and can only lead to resentment and relational pain. The reason the coaching frame is so unique and powerful for facilitating lasting change is because it is the only frame where there is no wanting or judgment (as you will soon see). The conversation has nothing to do with what the coach wants. It is entirely focused on what the other person wants.

Back to my kids. My best chance of actually being useful to them in the crucial years of their personal formation will not be by wanting them to be happy and make great choices. Instead, I need to be present for them, loving them for who they are and helping them to see that although they will make lots of good and bad choices, they are not defined by those choices. I get to show them that they will always have choices to make. Every passing moment comes pre-loaded with choice, more choice and even more choice. My job is to model what it looks like to make choices without being defined or judged by those choices. I have the opportunity to demonstrate a compelling and attractive life.

Everything else will be counter-productive to helping them on the journey.

As you enter the coaching space you will discover that I don't need anything from you and I'm not there to try and fix you. I won't lose any sleep over you or the choices you make. It's your life and you are the expert in your life, not me (this is one of the key distinctions between coaching and counselling or psychology—in coaching, the client is the expert, not the other way around). There is no right or wrong, good or bad. All that remains is what is.

Story

Sometimes people seek to identify with labels that define their experience of life. They may use language to describe themselves like: depressed, anxious, ugly, narcissistic, unmotivated, undisciplined and lazy. The issue comes when they attach their identity to these words. "I am (insert label here). These labels then become the program that they live out of and limit their experience of the world. They are a judgment from either self or others. In the judgment free space these labels are no longer useful. They become totally redundant.

Having people wanting things for us or from us is unavoidable, which is why having access to a space that is totally judgment free is so useful. As a coach I'm not going to be yet another person in your life who wants you to do something you don't want to do. My question to you is, what do YOU want? When you can tell me that, I'll give you every resource I've got to help you get more of what you're looking for. As a person who genuinely does care about others, it's not that I actually don't care about your issues or outcomes, but all my caring does absolutely nothing to bring about change. The truth is that no one has the ability to get a different result for you. Your results are totally up to you and it is essential that you know, see and own this.

Burning Wool

The initial development of my coaching toolset came through working with the long term unemployed. The company I created, delivered coaching to over 2,000 unemployed clients. We saw some amazing changes in people who had been written of by the system as too hard or too far gone. Our HOPE coaching program was described as being 'very safe and yet very confronting at the same time'. I think this beautifully expresses the power of the judgment free space created in the context of the coaching frame.

In the judgment free space you get to have incredibly real conversations, saying and hearing things that you certainly wouldn't get away with in any other space. When you really experience the freedom of no judgment, you are able to come out of hiding and be totally vulnerable without fear of being hurt. The cool thing about this is that when all the self-protection barriers come down, change takes place almost immediately. Until we're willing to accept where we currently are in life and become present to that reality, it is impossible to move to a desired reality. So often we hide behind a false reality for fear of being found out and judged.

When I was 12, my dad gave me an object lesson that has always stuck with me. As a wool classer by trade, he asked me if I thought wool would burn. I was pretty sure that it wasn't flammable so I was quite surprised when he held a match under a handful of freshly shorn wool and it immediately caught on fire. Equally amazing was the fact that the moment he took the flame away, the wool stopped burning. It turns out that wool cannot sustain its own flame. Paper on the other hand will continue to burn even after the initial flame is removed. His point was that so often this is what happens when we try to help others change or grow. It's all about our effort and energy. It looks like they are on fire, but all the energy is coming from us. The moment we stop giving input and doing what we're doing, the fire goes out.

I think this is why I was so taken by the coaching skillset the first time I saw it in action. Two weeks after being exposed to coaching I was in my first training intensive as part of a two year coaching diploma. Four weeks later I'd quit my job and launched my own coaching business! These tools are real, powerful and life changing. By remaining judgment free I'm not burning wool. From that place I can be entirely focused on equipping and empowering people, as the experts in their own lives, rather than creating codependent relationships that are incapable of producing change.

Like it or not, you are where you are. Your results are yours alone. Whether or not you 'could' or 'should' have done better is just useless, abstract speculation. Looking back is entirely unhelpful. You did what you did based on the level of thinking, awareness, beliefs and resourcefulness you had access to at the time. If you actually could have done better, you would have. Stop running and let yourself be found. Here's another helpful idea: you are not your behaviour. You are not your choices. You are simply doing the best you know how to do.

When there is no judgment from me, you will find yourself with the freedom to let go of self-judgment. We are often so quick to label ourselves and others by our behaviour, but when we view things through this frame, all labels fall away and all that remains is what is. To coach you from a judgment free space means that I will not be moved by your sad stories. There really is no value in me validating them or even wading into all the painful details. Of course stuff has happened to you (as it has to everyone). The only question that matters is; what do you want and what are you prepared to do about it?

Story is the enemy because it disempowers you and makes you a victim of your experiences. 'Story' is anything that allows you to justify letting go of responsibility and choice. For example:

"If A, B, or C hadn't happened then of course I'd be able to do X, Y or Z had, but it did, therefore I can't. I really have no choice in the matter."

The moment a coach buys into or validates your story, it is game over. You become a victim with no power who must make the best of their difficult situation. "If you just knew what has happened to me, you'd understand why I can't…"

When we get moved emotionally by someone else's story, it is not actually empathy or sympathy that is tugging at our hearts, we are simply trying their story on. It's reminding us of our story. We are placing ourselves in their shoes and feeling what it would be like if that was happening to us, or our kids/parents/friend/job/health etc. The moment we do this we become entirely focused on ourselves. We are no longer present for the person sharing the story, we are lost in our own story. As a coach, my commitment is to be completely present for you, with a heart to genuinely serve you 100%. I will not be moved by your story because I don't want to try it on. If I'm focused on me, I'm not focused on you and in that moment I lose all ability to be useful to you.

Don't confuse me for someone who cares

My goal is to hold the cleanest judgment free space possible. I remind my clients all the time to not confuse me for someone who cares. As coach, I genuinely do not care about the results they are currently getting in life. They cannot please or disappoint me. I have no vested interest in their results and no need to change them. I am NOT the one with the issue. I am however completely committed to serving them to get the results THEY say that they want.

To that end, I am here to hold the coaching space open and clean rather than imposing my judgments about what you should or shouldn't do to experience change.

Remember, contrary to popular opinion, caring is one of the least effective ways to facilitate change.

I am here to serve. You need to feel that and be totally convinced that I'm in your corner committed to get you more of what you want. At the same time, you genuinely need to feel that I do not care about your results, goals or problems. I don't care if you do the homework or not; if you deal with your issues or not; if you take responsibility for your life or not. I'm NOT the one with the issue.

Remember, contrary to popular opinion, caring is one of the least effective ways to facilitate change.

Questions

- *Which people in your world want certain things for you?*

- *How does their wanting make you feel? Does it produce lasting motivation for change?*

- *Which people in your life do you want certain things for?*

- *How do you think this wanting affects them?*

- *How high is your level of self-judgment?*

- *What do you imagine would be possible in your life if you let go of this self-judgment?*

- *Have you ever experienced the safety of the judgment free frame before where someone is totally focused on what you want rather than what they want?*

Chapter Two

BEING OUTCOMES FOCUSED

If you don't know what you want in life, you will end up serving the agenda of those who do.

COACHING IS ALL ABOUT OUTCOMES. THE MOMENT WE STOP talking about what YOU are aiming for, we are no longer having a coaching conversation. The two hardest questions to answer are the first two questions I'll ask:

1. Where are you now?
2. Where would you like to be?

The first question is so confronting because it requires honesty, vulnerability and self-awareness, it demands that you show up as the real you, not the you that you'd like to be. It is far safer to hide behind pretence and keep up appearances of happiness than actually face the painful reality of dysfunction and heartache. The judgment free space is the only space where it is safe enough to be real and come out of hiding. Whether you should or shouldn't be here doesn't matter, this is where you actually are.

The second question is terrifying because it opens up the very real possibility of failure, disappointment and rejection. It is also far safer to settle for what you can get than it is to boldly declare the dreams of your heart.

I recently ran a workshop on the idea of knowing what you want with a bunch of Year Eleven school prefects. I threw out the question, "What do you want?" and no one had anything to say. The funny thing was, I had asked a bunch of Year Three kids the same questions a few days prior and they all knew exactly what they wanted to be when they grew up! It's amazing that by the time kids have made it to senior high school they've already worked out that life isn't as easy as just having a dream and going after it. They've observed how those ahead of them are making a living and drawn the conclusion that the best plan is to just get by. By the age of sixteen, most of these kids have already made a decision to settle for what life dishes up to them rather than chasing what they want. That is a decision that is likely to remain that way for the next seventy years of their life!

Imagine going to your local mall and conducting a survey of the first one hundred people you came across. You ask them these simple questions: 'Excuse me sir or madam, are you clear about what you want in life?' and if so, "Are you actively chasing the dream?' I don't imagine that more than five out of those one hundred would answer yes to both questions. The vast majority (the ninety five) are probably just surviving in situations that they don't really want to be in.People's ability to remain in these less than ideal situations without changing them, really is astonishing.

I used to get surprised by how many people don't know what they want, but the truth is, it's just far safer to settle for what you can get, rather than to chase after what you want! However, if you don't know what you want, the only other option for your life is that you will end up serving the agenda of those who do. That's how the world works. The 5% of people who know exactly what they want, enlist the other 95%, to help them get it done!

If you want to succeed in life and not just survive, you've absolutely got to know what you want. More than that, you also have to be crystal clear on what happiness and success is to you. It is crucial to make the decision to own your dreams and to chase desires even though you may never get there. Without this internal drive around your dreams, goals and desires, it is inevitable to end up as a slave to someone else's dreams and desires for your life.

What do you want?

While this question sounds so simple, it really is anything but. In fact this is the most dangerous and important question we ever get to ask ourselves.

Interestingly, to desire is human. Each of us have built into our very DNA a sense of what happiness and success is to us, so to say that you don't know what you want, is to actually be pretending not to know.

If you were to become clear about what you really desire, that would bring you face to face with the chance for conflict, judgment, responsibility, failure, disappointment, stress and mistakes. Scary stuff!

Yet, it is still the most important question we ask ourselves. To suppress desire is to dehumanise yourself.

When it comes to the coaching conversation, everything revolves around this one question. It is the driver for all lasting change work in your life.

When you do give yourself permission to answer it honestly, here are some of the cool options you immediately open up:
- You can improve the quality of your relationships, finances and health
- You can attract higher quality people into your life who allow you to be you rather than keeping you small
- You can develop as a human being and reach your potential
- You learn so much about yourself and who you really are

- You can inspire others to live large and chase their dreams too
- You can to contribute your unique gifts and talents to the world
- You move beyond merely surviving and start thriving
- You can create a life you don't need an escape from

So, before you read on, pause and have a go at answering these key questions

- What do you want?
- Where would you like to be?
- What would you like to have happen?
- What results are you looking for?
- What would excite you?

Remember, that this is about you and your life. You are the expert here. You are the one looking for change and so you will need to be the one doing the hard work. If it feels like I am cajoling or convincing you to do or see something that you clearly don't want to see or do, we need to stop the conversation immediately. Why would I be working harder than you? I don't need anything from you... I don't care remember? I'm not the one looking for change. This conversation has nothing to do with the outcomes I want. It is all about serving your agenda and getting you more of what you want. If you don't want something different to the results you are already experiencing, then I have absolutely no value to add.

Being outcomes focused, we're not going to get stuck in your story, or feel sorry about it. The key is to focus on what it is you want rather than focus on the problem or what you don't want. Knowing what you want and why you want it is the ultimate leverage to get you out of your story. We've all had setbacks and had to deal with unfortunate challenges, trial, trouble, pain, hurt, misfortune, the bad behaviour of others, and unfair situations. You have every right to live out of that story and play that card as the reason why you can't, or it's too hard, or too late etc. The only problem with that story is that it can't serve you in getting more of what you want. You must leave it behind in order to reach for your future. Lose sight of your goals and smother your dreams at your own peril. It's a dangerous game to play, with serious repercussions.

Well-formed Outcomes

Once you're clear on the outcomes you're looking for, it's vital to make sure those outcomes are well formed. For example, 'I want to get fit' is not a well formed outcome because it can't be measured. What is fit? Fit according to whose standard? How will you know you are fit? When will you achieve this by? Abstract goals like this can never actually be achieved.

Doing life well is all about being very clear about the kind of life you desire to live.

Here is a great model from Dr Ian Snape, to help you set well-formed outcomes.

Outcome

a) What do I want? – What would I like to have happen?

The goals need to be stated in the S.M.A.R.T.E.R[5] format. Make sure each outcome is:

Specific,
Measurable,
Attractive,
Realistic,
Time bound,
Ecological, and
Resourced.

Intention

b) If I had that, what would that give me? What is the intention behind the outcome? Knowing the intention behind the stated outcome allows you to make sure that the outcome is actually the thing you really want. Interestingly when you start exploring the intentions behind your goals, you soon discover that it's never about the thing, it actually what the thing represents. That's super important to become aware of, because when you see what you really want, there may be 5 better ways of getting it than the one you've initially chosen. This also helps you to avoid becoming attached to a specific vehicle that may never actually be able to deliver what you really want.

Having a big 'why' is crucial for motivation. When the 'why' becomes big enough, the how takes care of itself.

People ask me all the time, do you know anyone who is as stuck as me who has found a way to overcome these challenges and move forward again?

Every time my response is – So how does it serve you for me to answer that question?

If I say no, that will confirm your fears that it is too hard and you are too broken. If I say yes, you will immediately be trying to work out how you are in fact different from them.

The only questions that matter are; – Do you want to change? Is it important to you? Are you willing to do whatever it takes? Great then be the first! Even if no one has found a way to get back in the game from the place you find yourself in, be the first.

Almost everything you enjoy in today's world was totally impossible at some point in history. Yet some bold creature got it in their head that the world needed their invention and then created a way for it to become possible. They brought into existence a solution that had never been conceived of before.

Remember, necessity is the mother of all invention. If you want it badly enough, you'll find a way to make it happen! Get clear about what you really want and why you are no longer willing to live without experiencing this in your life and you will discover what you are really capable of.

Consequence

c) What are all the consequences of getting this outcome? List ALL the upsides and downsides. Be careful what you wish for, because you just might get it!

Everything comes with a price. Exploring the consequence of achieving your dreams and desires is often the most neglected or overlooked part of the goal setting experience. Take these goals for example: I want a promotion. I want to win a gold medal at the next Olympics. I want to earn $200k a year.

They all sound incredible, and I'm sure they are…but they all come with a price tag. To gain the promotion may mean having to neglect your family; to win gold, may cost you your social life of and earning $200k could cost you having to be at your best 5 days a week rather than cruising through life only needing to perform for special occasions.

I'm not in any way trying to discourage you from chasing your dreams, just to make sure you weigh up the costs of change against the costs of staying the same. Everything comes with a price. You really can have whatever you want as long as you are willing and able to pay the associated costs.

The harder you work in setting up your goals, the easier they are to achieve.

This process means, that to the best of your knowledge you are fully aware of what you are signing up for before you press the go button on chasing a specific goal.

Once you've looked at these three areas, ask yourself if there anything you'd like to change. If not, you have a well-formed outcome that you can begin to action. If yes, there is more work to be done before you can confidently pursue the stated goal.

Questions

- *Are you the kind of person who gives yourself permission to ask the 'what do I want?' question, or do you find yourself living out what other people want?*

- *Do you have a clear list of well-formed outcomes that you are working towards at the moment?*

- *Have you ever experienced an example of a big 'why' causing you to create a solution that others said was impossible?*

Chapter Three

HAVING INCREASED AWARENESS

Awareness is 90% of the issue. If you can't see it, you can't change it.

It amazes me how little self-awareness most people have. They seem to wander around in a daze, just taking their cues about happiness and success from the masses around them, or the noise of the media. People rarely stop to ask decent questions about their own behaviour, or the results they're getting. It seems they just keep doing what they have always done, hoping that things will naturally improve or sort themselves out.

It always fascinates me how scared people seem to be about looking beneath the surface in their lives. It is as though they are terrified of the pain, doubt, hurt and insecurity they may find. To avoid this they constantly avoid any conversation or situation which may leave them vulnerable to being exposed.

If you are like many people embarking on a journey of personal development, you may associate self-awareness with a sense of pain or fear. From my experience this association will turn around very quickly as soon as you start to get a taste of the joy to be found in knowing yourself. Awareness leads to all the good stuff and becomes something you are unable to live without.

Becoming External

Self-awareness is the ability to be external to your own thoughts. Eckhart Tolle says that the ego is the source of our madness. He equates ego with the unobserved mind[6]. The simple act of becoming aware of your own thought processes and emotional state begins the process of dealing with the madness.

Think of a rookie truck driver who takes his rig to get fixed after hearing a strange noise under the hood. The expert truck mechanic is never going to say, "Buggered if I know what's wrong with the stupid thing." No, instead he will be supremely confident that he can find the source of the noise and fix it, every time, even if he's never come across that particular problem before. The mechanic is 100% certain that the answer to the problem can be known, discovered or uncovered. It's the same with people. One of the most common symptoms of poor self-awareness is when you hear yourself say 'I don't know...' A great way to move forward from that point is to ask 'what am I pretending not to know?' We can always find the answer as long as we ask the right question.

Two of the coaching industry's big hitters have some key things to say about the power of awareness. Anthony Robbins declares that the quality of our life is determined by the quality of the questions we ask ourselves.[7] Stephen Covey says that our ability to be self-aware is what separates us from animals. He says, we are not our feelings, moods or thoughts. The fact that we are able to think about these very things proves we are separate from them.[8] Mindfulness is simply the practice of being external to our thoughts. The simple act of becoming aware of our own thought process and emotional state separates us from the dysfunction of ego. In fact Tolle goes so far as to say that awareness is the opposite of ego.

The dispassionate observer

Did you know that it is impossible to do self awareness and self judgment at the same time?

When a person begins to reflect on their own behaviour in an attempt to increase self-awareness, often they do it as the critic or the drill sergeant. They imagine that shaming themselves, disapproving or trying to force themselves to toughen up and just get it sorted will bring about change. Yet the internal critic or the drill sergeant can never bring about lasting change because they come from a place of judgment. This causes us to shut down and hide which further suppresses the truth of what is really going on. One of the best ways to reflect on your own and life is as a dispassionate observer. That is; you have no agenda, no judgment, no opinion, you are simply curious.

When we create a judgment free space it becomes possible to simply be curious. An attitude of curiosity leads to high-quality questions, which leads to new levels of self-awareness, learning, growth and the potential for change.

The process of personal development and formation really centres around building the relationship you have with yourself, which is completely dependent on awareness. It's about discovering this beautiful 'aha' moment when you see what is really going on beneath the surface.

In a judgment free space, labels fall away. We are free to observe things with curiosity and wonder, without the need to reduce them to safe, known quantities by using labels. A great place to start letting go of labels is with our own body. When we experience something uncomfortable in our bodies we are naturally tempted to label that feeling as 'sickness', 'pain', an emotion or fatigue. Incredible new layers of awareness open up if you simply treat the 'something' as a signal. Be curious about it and ask yourself: 'What for?' [9]

Let me illustrate the power of awareness to facilitate better results.

Rapport with Self Through Awareness

I'm normally in bed before 10pm. Recently I'd had a busy week and found myself heading to sleep at 11pm. I was so tired I could hardly keep my eyes open while brushing my teeth, however, the moment my head hit the pillow I was all of a sudden wide awake. My heart started pumping and I felt anxious and tense. My immediate response was to get frustrated with myself for such a pointless way of behaving when I knew that all I needed was a good night's sleep. I started to fight against my anxiety, telling myself to hurry up and sleep because I had another big day tomorrow and couldn't afford such a crazy set back. After ten minutes of this unproductive strategy I realised it was getting me nowhere, so I decided to employ the opposite approach.

I stopped labelling it as anxiety. I stopped fighting it and asked, "what for?" I started listening. I asked my heart why it was beating so fast and enquired about the positive intention of the feelings my body was producing (As you'll discover in the 'people work perfectly' frame in the next chapter; EVERY negative behaviour has a positive intention. Therefore simply being curious about the 'what for?' is always a great place to start). To my surprise I heard myself say, "Thanks for finally asking… Actually, in the last two days there have been seven major things you've been processing and you haven't finished even one of those conversations, or made a plan for any of them. I'm worried that you'll go to sleep now and wake up tomorrow having forgotten about these important issues and it will take me six months to bring them to the surface again. I would hate for that to happen."

In my tired state, I tried to argue with myself, "But I don't know what the seven things are… I've already forgotten them."

"Just get up, get out your journal and your good pen and I'll show you all seven of them." I replied Amazingly, 20 minutes later I had recalled all the issues, made some key decisions about each area and developed an action plan for them. I went back to bed and straight to sleep.

Here's another story about self-awareness. I love to run. My body shape and build is suited to distance running and I'm not too bad at it. The marathon is the ultimate challenge for a distance runner and there's something almost spiritual about digging into the depths of what your body is truly capable of to complete the distance. I ran my first marathon when I was 23 and, as a result of pushing my body to the edge to accomplish it, I have had sciatica due to a tight piriformis muscle (bum cheek) ever since. In the last ten years I've run another five marathons, driven by the dream of climbing onto the podium at the Townsville marathon. Prior to the last event, I'd finished fourth on two occasions and had run times that would have won the event outright in previous years.

I entered the 2014 marathon fitter, faster, stronger and more mentally tough than ever before. This was going to be the year. I had trained incredibly well for almost nine months and had pushed my body to new levels in preparation for the race. A month out from the event my sciatica really started to flare up. Since my first marathon, I've consistently managed it through rigorous stretching, dry needling and massage, so I was accustomed to putting up with some regular pain. However, this time it was so bad I could hardly run at all. I'd already passed the point of no return and was desperate to utilise my great form, so I reduced my weekly kilometres and nursed my leg as well as possible to make sure I made it to the start line.

Come race day, it seemed like everyone in Goulburn—my home town—knew I was running (that may have had something to do with the fact that it was all I'd talked about for at least six months) and I received a huge number of messages of support and encouragement from friends and family. My mum and dad surprised me by flying up the night before, and my wife and kids were at the race for the first time.

I stood on the start line in the pre-dawn darkness, amongst the smell of deep heat and nervous athletes, ready to dig deeper than ever before. Waiting for the gun to go off, I got word that race officials had doubled the prize money and this had attracted a hotter field than ever before. 'Bang!' We were off and running. Just

50 metres into the 42.2km race I knew that my dream was over. Even on my very best day I was not capable of keeping up with athletes who were on the edge of national and Olympic selection. I finished 8th and ran considerably slower than I had trained. I battled a sea of rising disappointment and embarrassment each time I ran past my cheering family.

Six months later I had hardly run. My sciatica was worse than ever and I had this strange pain in my right foot. My initial way of dealing with the pain was to treat the symptoms. So I sought out a physiotherapist in an effort to fix the problem. Despite this, the pain was still there and I still wasn't able to run freely. In desperation, I figured it could be worth having another go at this idea of learning to listen to myself. I decided to start by having a conversation with my foot. No judgment, no labels, just asking "what for?" So I checked in with my foot and asked the same question as with my anxiety. "Foot…what is the positive intention in this pain you are producing?"

It answered me right away, "Well here's the thing Jaemin. I don't really like you at the moment. You punished me hard for the last nine months. That was one intense training regime. Rain, hail or shine we did double sessions, hills, sprints and long runs. I had blisters and was bruised and sore the whole time, but you told me to keep going and that it would be worth it. Well here's the news… It so wasn't worth it. We didn't achieve the goal you were driving so hard towards and there was no reward for all that pain. I don't want to go through that again. This pain is working really well for me, because it's stopping you from launching into the next crazy training program. Until you and I have a conversation and find a way forward that is sustainable and life giving, I will keep using this pain as my protection from your pain."

Trauma

Trauma is what happens when rapport with self gets broken. If you constantly turn off or ignore all the internal signals about what is not working and just keep sailing on, sooner or later the subconscious will revolt and sabotage the body so you are incapable of moving forward. Most sickness, anxiety, depression, weight gain, burnout and post-traumatic stress is self-generated by the subconscious due to a breakdown in the relationship with yourself. It's like the subconscious is saying 'you have stopped listening, you are living unsustainably and I am not OK with that any more so, for the sake of love, I will stop you by all means possible.'

When you remain in a situation that requires you to lie to yourself to make things work, it inevitably leads to trauma. Living out of a lie will eventually cause you to be at war with yourself as it violates the relationship between your conscious and subconscious.

Trauma is not caused by the terrible things we experience, it is caused by suppressing the human response to these terrible things and pretending that you are fine and everything is OK.

A great example of this concept is the PTSD experienced by many soldiers returning from war.

Army training is all about turning a human being into a soldier. The natural human response to life must be replaced with robotic obedience to the instruction of the commanding officer. This is not being critical of the defence force protocol; it is just how it has to be. It is dangerous for a soldier to be influenced by the natural human responses of compassion, empathy or fear when they are engaged in a battle situation. Those in charge must be 100% sure that their soldiers will only respond to orders and that the training will take over their normal decision making process.

A soldier must conform to the instructions from higher up the chain and are rewarded only for pre-programmed behaviour. That means all human response must be suppressed. The problem with this is that people are actually human beings not robots or machines. To suppress, ignore or turn off the best and most honest part of a person therefore, eventually creates some very real problems in the life of the individual. Ultimately this suppression of natural human response is the cause of trauma.

A soldier doesn't experience trauma because they see people killed all around them. They experience trauma because they see these things and are not able to have a human response to them.

Trauma happens when the relationship with yourself gets broken. To constantly turn off or ignore all natural emotions and internal signals is a cruel thing to do. Imagine if you treated another person in this way. When trust and communication become non-existent between the conscious and subconscious, sooner or later this leads to massive internal conflict. The subconscious says "I don't like it…" the conscious mind says "too bad, this is my job so I don't have a choice."

If the relationship stays broken, the subconscious has no choice but to finally override and remove the person from the situation all together. Out of the subconscious comes severe sickness, anxiety, depression, weight gain, burnout, or chronic fatigue as way of manifesting the internal trauma and giving a clear way out of the unsustainable situation. If you have PTSD, you no longer have to be a soldier.

I was working with a client who had frequently suffered all kinds of major illnesses over a seven year period, and they were increasingly getting worse. When we applied the awareness frame and had a look 'under the hood', she realised that she had stopped listening to herself because there was too much to prove to others. This debilitating series of illnesses was her body attempting to shut this crazy program down. As soon as she rebuilt the relationship with herself and started to listen and trust again, the sickness no longer served a purpose so she was able to let it go and return to full health.

The Gift of Pain

Pain is our most honest voice. It is a gift designed to protect us from further pain and tell us that we have incredible value and need to be protected. Pain tells us what is not right and informs us about the things that are unsustainable and emotionally damaging that need changing.

Typically we hate pain. We try to avoid, ignore, mask or run away from it at all costs. Most people don't listen to their pain because the moment we actually hear ourselves loud and clear, it demands we take action and make change. People would prefer not to face their pain and deal with the things that require massive action because it's easier not to. We believe we can't afford to listen. We are afraid that pain will only tell us to stop something that we're attached to. Although it is killing us, it defines us. Pain doesn't tell us about the future and what we should do, it simply tells us what is not working now. Not listening to pain is like turning off the warning lights on our dashboard or the light in the lighthouse because it is annoying us. When we do that, there is nothing to prevent the car from running out of oil or the ships sailing onto the rocks. Pain is simply an internal signal about something that is not right physically, emotionally or relationally. The purpose of this signal is to protect us from further pain by alerting us to the things that need changing immediately.

One of the most remarkable contributions on the subject is Dr. Paul Brand's book 'The Gift of pain'. His radical pioneering work with leprosy sufferers in India has revolutionized our understanding of the disease as well as our need to embrace pain as a gift from God. While most diseases are feared because of their pain, leprosy is deadly because its victims feel no pain. According to Dr. Brand, the destruction of facial features and limbs follows because the warning system of pain is gone. Because of the inability to feel pain, leprosy causes its victims to inadvertently destroy parts of their own bodies.

Brand tells the story of a two year old girl with leprosy who continually bit the end of her finger and drew on her sheets in blood simply because she could. It turns out that not feeling pain is rather dangerous.[10] If you put your hand too close to the heater, it is supposed to hurt. That's the signal to say 'please remove your hand from danger immediately.'

Brand says "I began to view painlessness as one of the greatest curses that can befall a human being… My esteem for pain runs so counter to the common attitude that I sometimes feel like a subversive, especially in modern Western countries. On my travels I have observed an ironic law of reversal at work: as a society gains the ability to limit suffering, it loses the ability to cope with what suffering remains… traditional cultures may lack modern analgesics, but the beliefs and family support systems built into everyday life help equip individuals to cope with pain."[11]

Becoming self-aware can seem strange or difficult if you have never made time to stop and listen to yourself. The great news is, you can learn. If you can't hear or see what's going on under the surface it is highly likely that you are attempting to have these conversations with yourself as the critic, the judge or the drill sergeant. It is likely you imagine that this hard line approach will change your behaviour, when in fact it only reinforces the danger of being vulnerable. Your inner self will resist this approach and put up more walls to hide behind.

Imagine sitting in front of someone you have never met before and asking them to tell you all about what's really going on in their life. Imagine also that your body language is closed, you are checking Facebook on your phone and you tell them you've only got five minutes so they better make it snappy. Do you think that they will readily open the vault and share their deepest feelings with you? I think not!

So what does it take for a stranger to open up? Every day, people come into my office whom I've never met before, and within two minutes they feel comfortable enough to tell me things they have never said out loud before. This happens because I carefully create a judgment free space for them and they sense the fact that I am only there to serve them. This makes it safe enough for them to access self-awareness, often for the first time.

It's no different when you are building a relationship with yourself. It is only as we create a judgment free space and listen to ourselves as the dispassionate observer that it's safe enough to be open and real. Let go of the judgment and watch how easy it is to see and hear what is really going on inside.

My former business partner Robert Holmes ran a successful podcast for a number of years interviewing leading thinkers in the coaching industry from around the world. One of my favourite episodes was an interview with NLP expert Dr. Ian Snape who is arguably the best peak performance coach in Australia. As a result of the connection they formed, I got the chance to meet Ian over lunch when the three of us were in Sydney. In a moment of boldness I asked him to mentor me and to my surprise and delight he immediately agreed!

For our first official mentoring conversation, Ian invited me to spend three days camping, abseiling, rock climbing and snorkelling for abalone on the east coast of Tasmania—which has to be some of the most extraordinarily beautiful country in the whole world. One of the key conversations we had was about my running and how to rebuild trust and rapport with my body after the disappointment and pain of the last marathon effort. His coaching work with me centred on developing an internal signal that would let my body clearly tell me where the limits of sustainable training were, so that I would be able to run again. My subconscious suggested that a burning sensation on the instep of my right foot would serve the purpose, so I made a handshake agreement with my subconscious that I would not run whenever the signal was on.

After three days of the most extraordinary conversations of my life, mixed with some truly magic first time experiences in picture postcard surroundings, Ian asked me if I'd like to go for a run as a way of integrating all the internal change work we had been processing. I checked in with my foot and got a green light. He dropped me off on an 11km wilderness track that led through steep mountains, across pristine beaches and took in some exquisite natural scenery. Half way around the loop I had to stop and turn my high tech running watch off. The constant display of speed, distance, heart rate etc. was anchored to high performance training and I felt I was breaking rapport with my body again. I sensed myself say, turn the bloody thing off and just be present. Run for the sheer joy of it. Rediscover the natural beauty of muscle and sinew doing what it was designed to do.

I completed the tough 11km off-road loop and then had to run another five kilometres down the road to meet Ian at a café for breakfast. It was a big effort considering I had not run for six months. Historically my sciatica flares up after running and sitting, so I was not looking forward to the three hour car ride back to Hobart after my one and three-quarter hour run.

During the drive, I asked Ian if he'd mind me being anti-social and taking some time to journal the key conversations we'd had over the last three days. He agreed that it sounded like a great idea, so I opened my notebook, removed the lid from my nice pen, put my earphones in and pressed play. This unlocked a sea of emotion and I bawled for 30 minutes straight. I have never experienced such incredible gratitude, beauty, peace, joy and personal congruence. When I emerged from the cloud and dried my eyes, I immediately noticed a strange tingling in my left bum cheek and realised that 13 years of accumulated tension in my piriformis muscle had been released. When we arrived back in town, I got out of the car totally pain free and have remained so ever since.

Arriving home a few days later, I was so excited that I had no pain or tension in my bum and no sciatic nerve pain down my left leg that I ran three days in a row… even though I had pain in my right foot. I totally ignored the signal and ran anyway.

After the third day of running I had a horrible dream that seemed to last all night. In the dream, my wife would not listen to me or understand a word I was saying to her. It was so infuriating and unfair. I couldn't believe the injustice of it all or how she could be so cold-hearted towards me! I woke up in a terrible state and the effect of the dream lingered with me into the day. That morning I had an hour long car trip to get to a meeting, so I took the opportunity to do a mindfulness exercise in an effort to change my state.

Suddenly I heard my internal voice say, "You do know what that dream was about don't you?" I really had no idea. My best guess was that it was about something my wife had done wrong. I was quite shocked to hear from my subconscious that the dream was about me. "We had a deal and you broke it on day one! The signal was on, yet you deliberately ignored it and violated our arrangement." Because I had been the victim in the dream, I was immediately able to totally associate with the pain I had caused myself by not listening or understanding. My internal voice went on, "I'm not trying to hurt you or hold you back Jaemin. You have no idea what we'd actually be capable of if we were to work together, rather than you just forging ahead with whatever seems best to you at a rational level!"

I sincerely apologised to myself and recommitted to our contract. Since that day, I always check in with my body before I run and on numerous occasions have had to put my shoes away and do something else because the signal is on.

I'm a huge fan of the T.V. series 'Breaking Bad'. It has to be one the most cleverly written pieces of drama in the history of the world. One of the minor characters is a former drug lord who, since suffering a stroke, has been almost totally paralysed. He's confined to a wheelchair and has very limited use of his body. He cannot talk, so he uses a bell fitted to the arm of his chair to communicate. If the conversation is framed in such a way that he can give a 'yes' or 'no' response, he can communicate clearly. If the answer is 'no', his finger hovers tentatively above the bell, and if the answer is 'yes', he strikes the bell once. It works perfectly for those who understand the system. But when he is moved to a new nursing home, where no one knows how the bell works, the bell system becomes broken. Imagine the nurses' frustration trying to work out what the bloody ringing bell is supposed to mean. He is equally frustrated because no one understands what he is trying to say. The end result is a bell that is ringing all day and making no sense at all.

People simply need to figure out the bell. "Hey Hector…do you want a chicken sandwich?"

"Ding."

"Ok, cool."

When everyone understands the signal, he only has to ring the bell once and then it stops.

What for?

The same is true with internal signals. If you get it and respond appropriately, the signal stops immediately. If you don't understand and try to fight against it or shut it off, it keeps going all day (week, month, year, or your entire life). Instead of labelling what is happening in your body as anxiety, pain, fatigue or something else, why don't you simply check in and ask 'what for?'[12] If you hear and understand it, the signal will stop. If you don't get what it is trying to say, the signal will keep going.

Awareness makes way for communication, connection, understanding and deep rapport. Lack of awareness produces inner conflict, frustration, confusion and eventually trauma.

You may be familiar with my 'One minute coach' radio segment on air around the country. When I began the process and had the opportunity to record the first of the segments, I had another interesting signal show up. In order to get each minute of recording right, it is important that I script out each sound bite. As it turns out, I'd left this script writing project to the last minute and had spent most of Sunday putting together the content for Monday's early studio session. I went to bed satisfied that I was ready to go. In the middle of the night I woke up with snot literally pouring out of my head. My first thought was to label it as sickness. Obviously I'm sick, I've come down with a cold or the flu. As I thought about it though, it simply didn't make sense. I didn't feel run down at all. So I checked in with myself and asked, "What for?"

"What are you thinking with the radio scripts?!!" my subconscious replied, "They're not finished. You didn't edit any of them. When you get to the studio in the morning and open your laptop, you will end up embarrassed and you will waste their time and yours because the scripts are not good to go. Get them right." Two hours later, with the job done, the signal switched off and I went back to sleep.

Then it happened again two weeks later. Snot in the middle of the night. "What for?" I asked myself again.

"Here's the thing Jaemin. You've been in a poor mood for a week now. Come on, you've had your pity party. I get that things didn't work out for you very well last week, but you've gotta get out of this funk man. It's time to let it go."

So, after checking in with my self to find out what would work best to change my state at 3am in the morning, I got up again, watched the final episode of season 4 of 'Breaking bad' while journaling and eating Vegemite Sao's. It was incredible!

I may have been tired the next day, but I was definitely back in the game.

Dealing With Fear

Awareness also plays a key part in dealing with fear. Fear by nature is highly irrational and subjective. This leads to people being held back by the fear of the fear rather than the actual things they say they're afraid of. For example, a child might struggle to get to sleep because they are afraid there is a monster under their bed. The parent knows that no such thing exists, that it's all in the child's mind. What the child is really experiencing is the fear of the idea that there may be a monster under their bed. They don't know for sure, they just imagine that it is real.

Awareness is like turning all the lights on, pulling the bed sheets back and actually looking under the bed to see what may or may not be there. If there is a monster, at least we now know what it looks like and that we need to avoid it or deal with it. But if there proves to be nothing there, then there is no reason for continuing to live in fear.

We all have highly illogical and irrational fears that hold us back from our dreams. What one person is afraid of, the next person thinks is a stupid fear. Funny thing is, when the shoe is on the other foot, and the same process is repeated, the first person thinks the thing the second person fears is just as crazy. Turns out, we seem to view other people's fears incredulously and take our own very seriously.[13]

Often the things we are most afraid of exist as a reality in our mind and what's worse is that they go unexamined. This enables them to turn into fire-breathing dragons ready to consume us at any moment. Having great awareness of these fears and actually exploring what is really behind them often results in the discovery that what looks like the shadow of a fire-breathing dragon is merely a couple of mice playing silly buggers with a torch.

People get paralysed by the fear of failure. Using the awareness frame, we can explore the actual, worst-case scenario rather than just the fear of what might happen. For example, let's say you have always dreamed of starting your own business but are afraid to because it might fail. What if you stopped and took the time to imagine what could really happen if things went very badly. What if it failed so badly that you ended up bankrupt? Would that be the absolute end for you or would the world go on turning? Could you find a way to rebuild, like countless others before you?

Developing Internal Signals

One of the most profound ways to let go of irrational fears is to develop a clear internal warning signal to let you know that you are actually in danger of experiencing what you are afraid of, rather than just worrying that you might be getting close.

For example, imagine you have been given a hire car on the edge of Canberra and told to make your way to Sydney as quickly as possible for an urgent meeting. Unfortunately, the fuel gauge in the car is broken and you have no idea how much fuel is in the car. Added to that, you are not familiar with the road between Canberra and Sydney and so you don't know how far away the next petrol station is. I'd imagine this would cause you to feel quite anxious and worried about whether you will make it to your destination.

However, if you were to jump in your own car, which you knew was full of petrol, had a working fuel gauge (plus a warning light that came on when you only had 100km before empty) and you knew that there were petrol stations all along the route no more than 80km apart (making it almost impossible to run out of fuel), there would be absolutely no reason for anxiety at all.

I was working with a client recently who had been experiencing some really cool success and happiness for the first time in his life, until his dad retired and moved in with him. At this point he started massively self-sabotaging his own journey. Through the coaching process, he discovered a deep subconscious fear that the dysfunctions he saw and hated in his dad, also lurked inside himself. If that were actually true, there was no point forging on toward success because inevitably it would all come crashing back to earth, just as it had done for his father. While he knew that this was a very irrational fear (as there was no evidence to suggest he was like his dad at all), the fear was still very real and was causing considerable damage.

Just like driving a car without a fuel gauge, he had no signal to warn him of danger. As a result he was experiencing fear and anxiety about what might go wrong with no way of telling if that was actually likely or not.

I invited him to check in with himself and invite his subconscious to give him a clear signal that would warn him if he were ACTUALLY about to behave in a way that was like his father. His signal was a unique tension in the bottom of his stomach. The moment he agreed on the signal, the anxiety and fear stopped and he slept with peace for the first time in six months.

The Answer is Inside You

There is no such thing as an unresourceful person just an unresourceful state of mind.[14] People are incredible. Our brain is still the most technologically advanced machine on the planet and is capable of more computations per second than anything mankind has created to date. This means that we already have all that we need inside us to deal with the challenges life throws our way, including the ability to create new resources, states, beliefs or whatever else might be required.

It is my sincere belief that our bodies crave health and wholeness. We have the capacity to heal ourselves physically, emotionally and mentally. Health and happiness is the default we return to when we let go of everything else. Whether you think you do or not, you do actually know what is going on. You know what you want and you know what's wrong. You have the answers. What you don't have, you can create. You are the expert in your own life. The journey you are taking as you read this book is simply about helping you see your own incredible resourcefulness and to identify the exact things that are limiting your capacity to flourish.

Lasting change

Often we imagine that change is like climbing to the top of a snow-capped mountain. We can barely make out the flag we are to capture on the peak from where we stand at the foot of the mountain. In order to get anywhere near the summit we would have to hike through dense bushland, then scale slippery rocks, ice and snow while battling winds and rain. We know we should be at the top, and we really want to be there but it all seems so daunting. There are no guarantees that if we begin the journey we will actually have what it takes to capture the flag. This metaphor is very demotivating and causes us to pretend we are happy where we are at the bottom of the mountain.

Achieving change in life is actually nothing like climbing a snow-capped mountain. It is much more like you are sitting on top of a big hill in a parked car with the hand brake on. You are right on the edge, and the flag representing the goal of desired change or growth is at the bottom of the hill. All that is between you and that flag is the hand brake. If you were to release the lever, the natural consequence would be that you would roll forward towards your target. Sure, there is still some work to be done in discovering exactly what is holding you back, but once you let go, there is no stopping you. You have all that you need inside you. All you need to do is release the hand brake.

Despite what most people believe, lasting change does not come about through increased discipline, effort, hard work, determination and focus. Instead it comes about through increased awareness, forgiveness, letting go, and giving yourself permission to thrive.

Fighting Against Yourself

So often we are fighting against ourselves and experiencing a lot of inner conflict. Part of us wants to move forward, while another part seems to sabotage our own success. The amazing thing is that we imagine success comes when we win the war against ourselves and finally subdue the misbehaving faculties. Just stop and think about that for a moment.

Imagine you are a business owner, or boss and your aim is to get the most out of your employees. One of your employees is not performing well and you decide you need to take action to make sure they pick up their act. You decide to call them in and speak your mind. The conversation goes something like this:

"I don't like you or trust you. If I leave you to your own devices I don't believe you really have what it takes to do a good job, so I'm going to ride, whip and micro-manage all you do because if I leave you to your own devices, you'll be lazy and unproductive."

How do you think that will go for you? You may get some work out of them if you are lucky, but it will only be a matter of time before that employee tells you where you can stick your job. You'd get a far better result out of treating them with love and trust, supporting and resourcing them and showing that you believe in them.

It is exactly the same when it comes to your relationship with yourself. You can flog yourself and get results through discipline, effort, focus and speaking like a drill sergeant, or you can work with yourself and develop a beautiful relationship based on respect and trust. Peace comes when all the parts of us are pointing in the same direction. This happens when we start becoming *aware* of the why behind what we are doing. We stop fighting against ourselves and start learning to understand the positive intention behind the seemingly negative behaviour we're exhibiting.[15]

Peace never comes through war. It comes through awareness and understanding. Awareness becomes possible through holding a judgment free space. When there is no judgment it becomes safe to see what is, rather than live out of the falsehood of what should or shouldn't be.

Pretending Not to Know

Awareness clashes directly with the 'I don't know' response. People often pretend not to know what they want or what is really limiting them. When the light is turned on, it becomes possible to see and know ourselves. Complexity and isolation thrive in the shadows. When you step into the light, simplicity and commonality emerge. I love the question: "What are you pretending not to know right now?" from Susan Scott's book, fierce conversations.[16] As long as it is asked in a judgment free space, a high-quality, hard hitting question like that will always lead to greater awareness.

The advantage of staying in the dark and pretending not to know, is that you don't have to do anything. The moment you say out loud what you know to be true, this knowledge demands a response.

Stepping Outside of Ourselves

Awareness gives us the ability to step out of our completely subjective experience of the world and be much more objective about our reality.[17] One of the simplest and most effective ways to solve relationship conflict is to step away from the 'first person' position we live in and try on the 'second person' (other), and 'third person' (disinterested observer) positions. Trying this will bring increased awareness. For example, imagine you are having an argument with someone. You being you is 'first person', the person you are fighting with is 'second person' and 'third person' is the position of a bystander with no agenda. Most often we only see the world though our own eyes (i.e first person). But imagine stepping out of your body and having a look at the conflict through the eyes of the other party. Consider how they would be feeling and what they would be seeing. What insights could you gain about the situation that you were previously oblivious to? Now imagine stepping into the shoes of a disinterested bystander who has no agenda other than to observe what is going on. What would you feel or see, looking at the conflict though their eyes? Becoming aware of the second and third person viewpoint of our situation always gives us more choice about how to experience what is happening in our life. It makes us more aware, and less able to pretend not to know.

When you think of becoming aware, think of curiosity, objectivity, high-quality questions, discovery and rapport with self.

Questions

- *Is self-awareness in your life linked to pleasure or pain?*

- *What are you pretending not to know?*

- *What is dangerous about discovering what you really know?*

- *How would you describe your relationship with yourself?*

- *Have you ever considered pain as a gift before?*

- *What pain are you attempting to ignore at the moment?*

- *What might you discover if you stopped labelling things as sickness, fatigue or anxiety and asked 'what for?' instead?*

- *What are the most high-quality questions you could ask yourself?*

Chapter Four

PEOPLE WORK PERFECTLY

Our current results are the exact results we have designed our system to produce.[18]

WHEN IT COMES TO CHANGE, THE MOST COMMON APPROACH is to just stop it, try harder, be better, more disciplined, focused and energized. The default of resorting to behaviour management strategies to improve the quality of life is entirely ineffective and can never work long term. The common thought process is that despite having tried many times before, the only reason you haven't succeeded yet is that you haven't tried hard enough or long enough. All you need to do next time is try harder. That is bound to work! This approach overlooks the fact that behaviour is the thing that turns up at the end of the assembly line in the factory of your life. It is not created in a vacuum. It is produced by a whole bunch of internal frameworks and systems that you have subconsciously created to serve a clear purpose.

Bandler and Grinder, the co-founders of NLP in the 1970's, taught us that people are not broken, needing to be fixed. They held the view that people work perfectly.[19] The results we are getting are the exact results we have designed our system to produce. Our behaviour is never random, coincidental or strange. It is the final product that comes from our system of meaning and beliefs. When we understand that people work perfectly we totally eliminate behaviour management as a strategy for change.

Putting Sides on Boxes

If you went to a factory that was producing boxes and noticed the first box on the conveyor belt was missing a side, you'd probably jump to the conclusion that it was broken. If, however, you then observed that every box came out missing the same side, you'd have to believe that they were being created like that.

If what you actually wanted were boxes with all the sides on, you would only have two options for accomplishing that outcome: fix all the boxes or change the machine. Sadly, most people take the 'fix the box' approach to their personal change work. The trouble is, there's no end to the production line. Every box comes out needing to be manually fixed and that becomes exhausting. Some people seem to have more energy and capacity for putting sides on boxes than others, but ultimately it's a fool's quest.

It's futile to judge the box for missing a side, and futile to try and repair every box. If you want a different result, the only effective long term solution is to change the settings on the machine that is producing the result in the first place. When you change the machine the end result automatically changes. The box-making machines in our lives are our perceptions and beliefs. If you change your beliefs your behaviour will take care of itself.

Of course

People often have such limited awareness about why they behave the way they do. In the absence of this understanding, they commonly resort to self judgment and beat themselves up for behaving poorly. When the coaching conversation about this behaviour begins, I frequently respond with my favourite phrase, "Of course..."

"Of course you are overweight, sick all the time, unmotivated, have no friends, have chronic fatigue, can't make a decision... What did you expect? This is the exact result you have designed your system to produce and it is working perfectly!" Understandably, to them it doesn't *seem* like its working perfectly because the boxes look broken. But in reality, it must be working perfectly because it is consistently producing the exact same results.

I once coached a lady who was really overweight and desperate for change. She told me that she had tried everything over the last ten years to get her weight under control but had failed miserably every time. Now she was filled with self-hatred about her own appearance. I calmly responded with, "Of course you're overweight. In fact you obviously need to be fat! No one is putting food in your mouth. This is clearly working very well for you." (Try saying that to someone outside the coaching frame and see what happens! Obviously I had established a judgment free space with her first, otherwise there was no way I would have gotten away with saying that. I personally don't care if she is overweight—that doesn't affect me. I don't need her to be anything other than she is. She was the one who said it was a problem, not me).

It turns out that when she was in her early 20's she was slim and happy with her appearance. Then she suffered two really traumatic experiences at the hands of men. The pain of those experiences were so huge that subconsciously she designed a clever strategy to make sure that would never happen again. 'If I make myself unattractive, then no one will come close enough to ever hurt me like that again.' What a great strategy! It was working perfectly at accomplishing her secondary agenda. It wasn't safe to lose weight. And so every time she tried diet and exercise, her self-protective subconscious sabotaged the process and her weight loss program failed. Of course...

The moment she changed her beliefs about herself and about 'all men', she no longer needed to hide behind the weight to protect herself. Having made it safe to be thin again, she could let the weight go.

Flowing on from the 'judgment free' and 'self-awareness' parts of the coaching frame, the 'people work perfectly' premise helps us to understand more about the positive intention in all our behaviour and causes us to move away from behaviour management as a strategy for change.

Secondary Gain

When you come to terms with the fact that people work perfectly, it allows you to get to the bottom of what is really going on very quickly.

Underneath the game changing 'people work perfectly' presupposition, is a fantastic piece of psychology called 'secondary gain.'[20] Here's how it works:

So often, the stuff happening in people's lives is not the way they'd like it to be.

Yet the reality is - every single thing we tolerate or complain about but don't change must be working for us. On the surface it looks like we are losing, yet the reason we stay in that place is that underneath there is a gain, reward or payoff.

Primary loss...Secondary gain. The situation appears to be all bad, yet the hidden benefits keep up coming back for more.

It's classic Dr Phil: Someone comes on his show complaining about how bad their life is. He asks, "So how is that working for you...?

"It's not" they say, "weren't you listening? Let me tell you again how unfair and horrible it is…"

His reply is always the same. "Well clearly it is working, otherwise you wouldn't still be doing it! You are not that dumb.

You may do something once for no reward, but not twice and most certainly not for 20 years!"

In all my years of coaching, I'm convinced this is the hardest and most confronting piece of self-awareness work. This is because secondary gain ultimately protects you from the thing you are most afraid of about yourself. The most significant and therefore hardest to remove secondary gains are always about safety. We remain in our dysfunction because it protects us from failure, disappointment, rejection or being found out as somehow inadequate.

At the basic foundation of human behavioural science is the fact that we only do things that work for us. If something gives zero reward or gain, then we simply will not do it again. The implications of this one idea are staggering. I talk to many people who tell me how bad their situation is and how terrible their life is because of this, that or the other. They claim that if they had a choice they would be somewhere else, doing something else, but in fact, they are exactly where they have chosen to be!

I can't overstate how important this one concept is in the overall coaching process. Let me illustrate this principle with a very practical example.

Pick something hard that you would quickly come to hate doing.

For example, imagine you were sitting on the ground in the hot sun with a chisel and hammer, breaking rocks into smaller pieces and that you had to do that task all day. Now, I'm sure you'd agree that this would be very painful and difficult. The only possible reason you would continue with it is if you gaining some reward.

This reward could be physical, emotional, relational or financial, but on some level you must be aware of what it is. The absolute worst-case scenario is that you are in some kind of concentration camp forced to do hard labour, whereby the only payoff may be that you don't get killed.

The point is no one would just split rocks. The basic human drivers of pleasure/pain and reward/punishment demand that our efforts produce some benefits. Otherwise they are impossible to sustain. Without a reward of some kind, there is absolutely nothing to keep you picking up the hammer.

The same is true for every behaviour. It is impossible to do things you hate if you are not benefiting from the action at the same time. The reward may be hidden or hard to see, but it will always be there. It is incredibly offensive to suggest to someone that they are profiting from the things they least like in their life. Yet, there is no way around this hard-hitting truth if they want to experience freedom from their dysfunctions.

Being unaware of the rewards of living in dysfunction is a major hindrance to lasting change. Until you become aware of the payoff you get for living in a place you say you don't like, you will ultimately keep gravitating back to it simply because it works.

If the problem is that we are broken and need fixing, then again this makes the challenge of overcoming limitations incredibly complex and totally unique. But if we are not broken and in fact work perfectly, then the cause of our results can be seen, understood and changes made to improve them. Behaviour is not produced in a vacuum. It is the direct product of what we believe.

What a relief that we are not stuck with the 'only choice' of constant box fixing (working harder)! We can actually fix the machine making boxes in the first place!

Here is a great example of how powerful the 'people work perfectly' idea is when it comes to facilitating real and lasting change. One of our coaches shared the story of a couple she had been working with as a counsellor, prior to doing her coach training with us. She had spent five years digging into the depths of their challenges without any change at all. It was so fascinating for her to look at the same story through the coaching frame.

At 18, the client had fallen in love with a young man in the church she had grown up in. The couple were married the following year. By the time she was 23, she had given birth to their third child. Soon after, for some unknown reason, her husband had some kind of mental breakdown and became quite violent and abusive toward her. The situation escalated quite quickly and she ended up leaving the marriage for the sake of her children. So at age 25, she was a divorced single mother of three. She remained in the church congregation while he left and was not heard from again.

A year later a young man moved to the area and started attending the same church. He fell in love with the divorced woman and developed a relationship with her. Eventually she agreed to marry him, but on her wedding day became seriously ill. She has been ill ever since. For 20 years, her new husband has cared for her and has basically raised the kids on his own. These roles required him to quit his job so that he could focus on being there for his new family. The church family constantly prayed for the woman to be healed, and after 15 years of sickness she was miraculously cured. Six months later however, the sickness returned and, at the telling of the story, she was still sick.

Without any judgment, simply being curious and using the knowledge that people work perfectly, let's make a few key observations about this story:

- Growing up in a Christian culture probably instilled in the client a belief in the sanctity of marriage and that divorce is a sin.
- At 25 she has already blown her 'one chance' at marriage. It is most likely that she experienced high levels of self-judgment about this outcome, imagining that those in her church community were also judging her. She was probably asking herself, "What kind of a person gets divorced so young and causes three innocent children to grow up without a father? It could only be a bad person…"
- When the new relationship started it is probable that she believed she didn't really deserve to be happy and so subconsciously she set out to sabotage the second marriage before it even began.

- Falling sick on her wedding day was an interesting coincidence that suggests she was running a very deep protection strategy. Her first husband ended up abusing her and leaving her. By being sick she could ensure that her second husband would be highly unlikely to do the same. What kind of a man would neglect a sick woman?
- Perhaps she felt like a failure as a mother. By being sick, she could hand over responsibility of the kids to her new husband.
- Sickness made it more likely that she would receive pity from her church community, rather than judgment for being a bad mother.
- Her first husband had ultimately rejected her. If her second husband ended up doing the same, even after all the preventative measures she had put in place, he would only really be rejecting the 'sick her'. The 'real her' had never fully shown up to the relationship anyway.
- Now before you go feeling sorry for husband number two ask yourself, 'What kind of man pursues a recently divorced mother of three toddlers?' A rescuer. He's the hero in the story and a hero needs a victim to rescue. Imagine how much admiration this guy gets from the church community for being such a loving caring man under such difficult circumstances. He's probably won the 'Father of the Year' award ten years straight! People most likely stop in the street just to tell him how wonderful he is. Although he often complained about having to put his life on hold and having to quit his job, the payoff was enormous.
- At year fifteen, when she miraculously recovered from the sickness, neither of them knew what to do with the freedom and so they chose to go back to the old story that had been working so well.

We are not broken and we don't need fixing. Our behaviour is not strange, random or coincidental. It always serves a purpose.

Everything we do is in some way an attempt to bring peace and comfort to ourselves.

One of the most beautiful things about understanding this is that it allows us to separate behaviour from intention. Often we label ourselves and others by our behaviour, yet viewing our situation through the coaching frame allows the labels to be 'peeled off' and lets the intention be understood. is makes way for a new strategy to be designed that meets the original intention of the old behaviour AND is also in line with our core values[21].

Self discipline vs self permission

Self discipline is massively overrated. I get that it is the go-to strategy for producing better results, but there are far better ways of improving the quality of your life.

Self discipline is entirely about working hard. It is fighting against yourself as though the parts of you were bad or wrong or broken. It is an attempt to conquer yourself and suppress the dysfunction and pain lest it come out and destroy your efforts at moving forward. It is driven purely out of the conscious mind using the limited resources of willpower as the only means of strength. Self discipline always appears to be working for you, yet it never can produce lasting results. It is simply a behaviour management strategy.

One of the most common and also most unhelpful myths about success is that is totally connected to how hard you are prepared to work; Try harder, be better, use more discipline, energy, focus, commitment, drive, passion. Yet willpower as a panacea is massively overrated. Willpower is like a muscle. It gets tired and runs out.

Often people use it as a behaviour management tool to cover up the bad fruit their life is producing rather than to actually deal with the root cause of the problem. Some seem to have more will power than others, yet at some point it will inevitably run out. Self permission on the other hand is about making peace with yourself. It is recognising that all the parts of you (even the ones that feel like they are at war) actually want the same thing. Everything is driven from a sense of protection and love and wanting the best for you. It is about valuing the beauty and gold that lies within you. It is to honour your own wisdom and intuition. It is to build great rapport between your conscious and subconscious so that you find a way to work with yourself rather than against yourself.

Self permission is realising that ultimately you are the only one powerful enough to get in the way of your own dreams and hold yourself back, and you are the only one with the power to cause you to succeed. It is to take the handbrake off and allow yourself to be successful. It is to stop hiding your light under a basket and conform to how the world wants to you be. It is the willingness to fully show up in the world in all your uniqueness and to shine for all to see. When you give yourself permission to flourish there is nothing strong enough or big enough to get in your way.

Questions

- *Have you experienced the frustration of behaviour management strategies that don't bring about lasting change?*

- *What things are you complaining about or tolerating that you haven't changed?*

- *What do you think the payoff for not changing them might be?*

- *If you let go of self-judgment and were simply curious about your own behaviour what might you discover?*

- *What do you think would happen if you started working with yourself (self permission) rather than against yourself (self discipline)?*

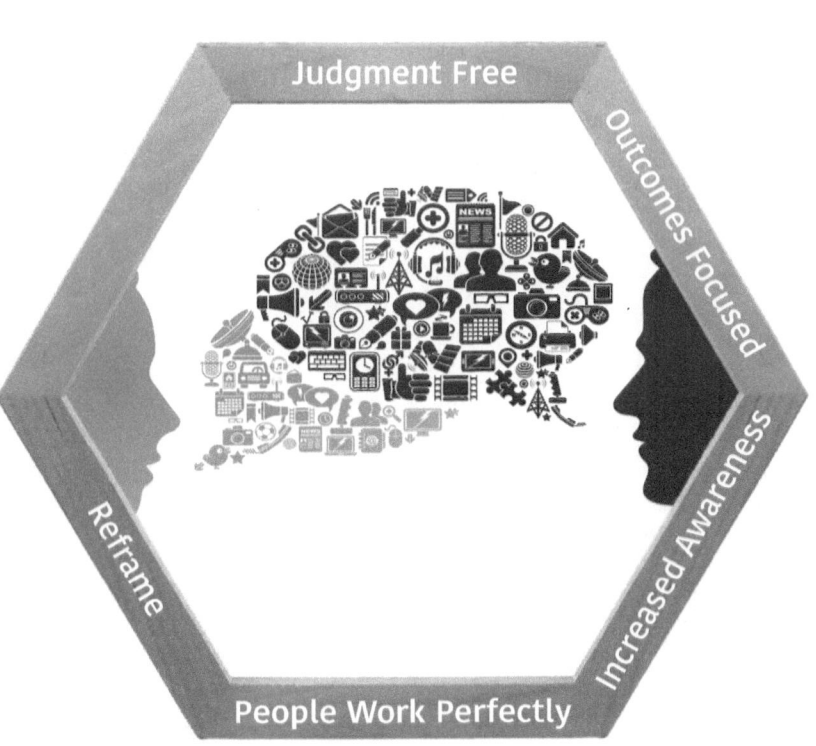

Chapter Five

EVERYTHING CAN BE REFRAMED

Everything can be re-framed because everything is framed in the first place.

I THOROUGHLY ENJOY EQUIPPING PEOPLE WITH THE COACHING skill-set. In one of the many training events I've run, a student who was struggling to come to terms with the implication of the content to her life asked this fantastic question: "Can everything be reframed?"

I replied that wonderfully the answer is yes…of course, because everything is framed in the first place.

We don't actually get to see reality. Instead, everything we experience in life is based entirely on our perception of that reality. We think we see the world as it is; yet five people observing the exact same event will all perceive and experience it differently. Eckhart Tolle says that the primary cause of unhappiness is never the situation, it is our thoughts about the situation.[22] The problems in our life are not the problem. The problem is what we think about the problem. Today's problem in the light of today is massive. The same problem in the light of this year is not as big, and it is most likely that this problem, in the light of your entire lifetime, disappears almost completely.

As I have mentioned previously, we see the world through a lens or a frame. It filters our experience of life and colours our understanding of what is actually taking place. When you change the frame you are looking through, you change your experience. We are convinced that what we see is entirely real and true… and to be fair, by our experience, it is. However, we realise it just may not be when we see that someone else, looking at the same situation, experiences it entirely differently and they are equally convinced that what they see is real and true. The human brain is an extraordinary machine. Every second it receives two million bits of information to process. Being unable to process every individual piece of data, it is constantly deciding what to filter in and what to filter out.

Our beliefs become the key factor in how our brain knows what to pay attention to and what to delete (ignore), what to distort (so it fits our mental picture), what to add back in (because it appears to be missing) and what to generalize (stereotype).[23] We find evidence for whatever we believe is true and that ends up being all we can see. Our beliefs become the frame through which we perceive our reality. We do not have the capacity to simply see what is really there. We are constantly filtering. We cannot stop filtering. Imagine having to be present to everything that is going on all the time. That's a recipe for an instant meltdown. Our brain takes shortcuts to help us manage our world and prevent information overload. We don't have time to process every individual thing to see whether it is safe and trustworthy, so we rely on the established patterns and biases in our brain, that have formed as a result of previous experiences.

I remember my brother being sick with a gastro bug when we were kids. He was feeling fine in the morning and devoured a big bowl of watermelon for morning tea. A few hours later his insides were churning. For the next 20 years he didn't touch watermelon again. His brain linked the horrible experience of being violently ill with this specific fruit, when in fact it was an infection. Obviously it wasn't the watermelon that made him vomit, and even if that particular watermelon had for some reason been the cause of his sickness, that doesn't mean every piece of watermelon in the future would produce that same result. However, his brain decided that it was the watermelon's fault, and this changed his interactions with the fruit for the next two decades.

This same process happens constantly as we interact with people, places, things and ideas. The frame or filter gets set, and we see things exactly the same every time.

Reframe Safety

One of the most significant examples of the power of reframing is in the area of personal safety. Human beings are wired for safety; it is part of our DNA. Our limbic system is responsible for protecting us from any perceived threat of danger. You've perhaps heard of the four 'f's' before? Our freeze, flee, fight and sex responses are driven by this system. You can't turn it off even, if you try.

Often people believe that those who succeed in life do so because they have less fear, more courage and don't need to feel safe. That is simply not true. When we start to think about chasing our dreams, we sometimes imagine that we simply need to be courageous and go for it. I reckon that's just like taking all your clothes off and running naked out into the street screaming, "I'm freakin' awesome!" You'll only ever do it once. That level of vulnerability and exposure is so threatening to your safety, you will make internal vows to never ever do anything like that again.

If turning off the need for safety is not the answer, how does a person ever overcome their internal inhibitions and fear of stepping out? This is where reframing comes in. It's all about having a closer look at what is actually dangerous.

Our subconscious sometimes behaves just like an overprotective parent. Motivated purely by love, an overprotective parent wraps their child in cotton wool so that they don't get hurt by the big bad world. They instil a sense of fear in the child about anything outside the safe, happy family environment. However, at some point as the child grows older, they begin to realise that the big bad world isn't actually as big and bad as they had been led to believe. They get the message that there are certainly some dangerous things in the world, things that can potentially cause a lot of damage. However, where they used to believe that all danger was outside the safety provided by family, they begin to realise that the opposite is actually true. Sure, there are some risks and hazards associated with living in the real world, but home is actually more dangerous. They come to see that mum and dad are the most dangerous people in their world. Sure they need protection, but protection from what? Their parent's overprotection is ruining their social skills, undermining their resilience and personal confidence, and creating an unhealthy dependence. They ultimately realise that the safest thing they can do is leave.

Likewise, our subconscious strategies for self-protection are well intentioned and yet they often end up achieving the opposite outcome. The most crucial step to really living is to interrogate our perception of safety and become aware of the genuine threats to our health and well-being.

I vividly recall a conversation with a man looking to do coach training with our company. He was very keen to begin, but he identified himself as a very risk averse person. He admitted that he had a really safe and consistent job and although he hated it, he couldn't envision ever leaving it to pursue the dream of a career focused on helping people. He imagined that the way forward required that he cast off fear and step out into the wild, which seemed unthinkable, even though he believed life coaching to be a good fit for him. It felt like running down the street naked. The breakthrough came when he reframed his idea of safety.

He saw a fresh perspective when I pushed back on what he saw as the strength of his risk aversion. I told him that if he were my risk manager I would fire him immediately because he had only ever done half of his job. He was good at assessing some risk, but completely ignored a whole range of other, more significant risks. He could clearly see the risk of leaving a comfortable job to venture out into the unknown, into a new career that he may or may not be any good at. But he had never assessed the risk of not stepping out. I asked him to put some work into assessing the risk of staying where he was. What was the likely cost to the state of his emotions, relationships and thought life? What was he risking by rocking up to a job he hated every day for 20 years? What was the risk in suppressing his dream every day for that amount of time? What about the risk to his kids who watched him trundle off to a dead end job every day even though he told them to follow their dreams? What was the risk to his marriage and his health? What about the risk to all the people who will never benefit from him at his best as a coach?

After a full risk assessment, he was startled to discover that the option of staying small and sticking with his safe job contained loads of risk. The far less risky option was to leave his job and pursue a career in coaching. As soon as he realised that he still got to stay safe while pursuing his dream, it changed everything.

People who flourish in life still have fear and will always be driven by the need to be safe just like every other less successful person. They just fear a very different set of things and are aware of very different threats to their safety. They are deeply afraid of anything that is going to undermine their sense of self, keep them small and needy or leave them with regrets and disappointment.

Reframe Success

People who succeed in life do so largely because of the stories they live out of. They realise that it's just a story and so the moment the story stops working, they pick a better story. It's common for people to frame success as difficult, rare and out of reach for the average person. I don't believe that story will actually help me succeed. Instead, I choose to tell myself that to succeed in life is actually easy, because most people never will! Doing a few key things well more often than not quickly causes you to rise above the crowd.

I'm not sure that there is anything more beautiful than seeing a person really find themselves and live an authentic life. I've come to notice that the rare people who do life well, tell better stories than the multitudes who just get by. Hellen Keller demonstrated this, saying that life is a daring adventure or nothing.[24] Joseph Campbell is credited with saying, "The cave you fear to enter holds the treasure you seek."[25]

Stories are what we live out of to make sense of our life. We tell ourselves and our children stories about God, money, family, friends, happiness and success. One of the biggest challenges about these stories is realising that they are indeed stories. They are works of fiction, metaphors, frameworks and sense making paradigms that can always be changed, developed or discarded and recreated to suit our purposes. We get to choose our stories and that means we get to decide how we experience our life.

Reframing Questions

1. *What's the gift in this?*

Anthony Robbins says that if you trade your expectations for appreciations, you'll immediately feel grateful. And it's when we're grateful that we feel rich and wealthy, regardless of how our lives look financially or materialistically.

2. *How can I use this to get more of what I want?*

When you focus on your desired outcomes, rather than your problems or failures, it allows you to see things that you once perceived as limitations, as opportunities to get more of what you want now.

3. *What would a freakin' legend do in this situation?*

Imagining you are someone else gives you access to a very different set of resources to deal with your current situation, which then opens up access to very different results.

4. *What must they believe in order to behave this way?*

Seeing the world through someone else's eyes, by stepping into their shoes, always allows you to gain new insights that lead to more choice and new experiences.

5. *What would a complete stranger, with no agenda or attachment, observe about this situation?*

If your only aim was to be curious about your current situation, what would you notice that you have not been able to see before?

6. *What, how, when specifically?*

Fine tuning your focus to pay more attention to the specific details will allow you to see things that were previously blurry or hard to define.

7. *Why? For what purpose? What does that give me?*

Lifting your eyes up, out of the detail, to get clear on the overall intention or purpose of what you are ultimately trying to achieve increases motivation and gives big picture vision. The details of how you're going to get there become insignificant when you're focused on the passion of your big dreams.

8. *In 20 years how will I feel about this moment/issue/decision?*

Hindsight is a wonderful thing. This reframe helps you go out into your future and look back on your current situation to see how it will feel from that position. Time heals all things.

9. *What if you only had six months to live?*

Taking away the luxury of an open-ended timeframe totally changes how you feel about the current situation and the decisions you need to make. For instance, if you knew you were going to die in the near future, how would that affect the way you lived today?

10. *What is the lesson here?*

What if your only objective was to learn more about yourself, others and how the world works? In this reframe, there is no failure only feedback.

11. *What if I'm the problem?* [26]

Try giving the problem to a couple of other people and see how they would approach it. Maybe you can't see the answer because you are in your own way.

12. *What if I don't fix this, and just move on?*

Is this a problem that actually needs to be solved or have you become emotionally invested in solving a problem that will actually have no real effect on your life or business if you don't solve it?

13. How can I break this down into smaller parts?

Breaking a problem down into smaller parts makes it less intimidating and gives a sense of progress as you solve each part incrementally.

14. Are my constraints real?

Are there self-imposed constraints to your situation? Are the things holding you back from solving the problem actually real or are they based on beliefs, ideas or rules that are not even true anymore?

15. What if I pick a better story that gets me more of what I want?

What other story could you tell yourself that would totally change this situation? Rather than focusing on whether the story is right or wrong, ask yourself whether or not the story is useful? Is it getting you the outcomes you want?

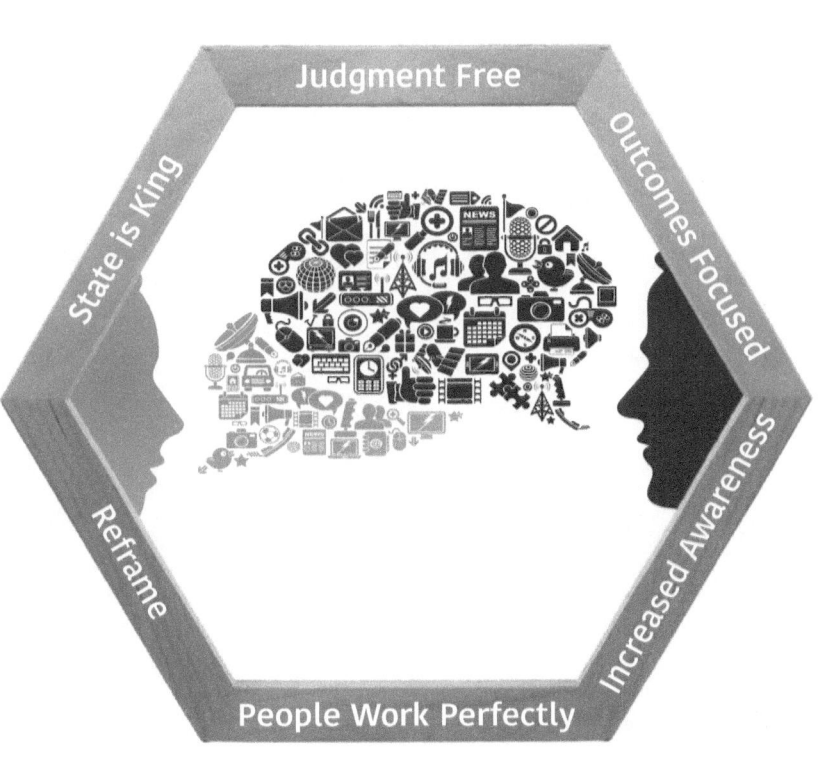

Chapter Six

STATE IS KING

"If you can control your state, you can control your outcomes."[27]

Having clear outcomes is so critical to your capacity to move forward in life. Therefore, the most important question for you to answer is always - 'what do I really want?' If you don't know what outcomes you are looking for, then how do you know there is anything wrong with the ones you've currently got?

My bet is that as soon as you get clear about what you want, you will instinctively jump to the HOW question. You will want to figure out what to DO to get what you want. The problem with this strategy is that often 'doing' is not enough. You may put a plan in place and work very hard but, despite your determination and persistence, you just don't seem to be able to make it. You get close, but not close enough. You hit a brick wall. It doesn't matter how hard you work, you just don't have access to that outcome. You end up with a feeling of frustration and hopelessness.

It might be surprising to realise that more often than not, it is your mental and emotional state of being that determines whether or not your desired outcomes are even possible.

State is King

State is king. It is the thing that most determines the results you get in every area of life. If you can control your state, you can control your results. The state you are in right now is the thing determining what internal emotions, thoughts and resources you have access to and which ones you don't. There really is no such thing as an unresourceful person; just an unresourceful state.[28] When you're in a resourceful mental and emotional state, time almost becomes irrelevant. What you can do in just one hour in a great state, may take you all week in a poor state!

Being in a great state, being in the zone, being on fire, experiencing flow—or whatever you want to call it—opens up a new realm of possibilities. Outcomes are simply the fruit of possibilities made available by the state that you are in at any given time. If you pay attention you will notice that any given state will open up a range of possibilities while making other things impossible. Every state has open and closed doors associated with it. For instance, a great state may make creativity, influence, confidence and intuition possible and things like procrastination, anxiety and laziness impossible.

The process of writing this book that you are currently reading is a great example of state management. My well formed-outcome was to write a high quality personal development book and have it published within twelve months. I knew exactly what I wanted and why I wanted it, yet I consistently found that the biggest factor in actually achieving this outcome came down to my state. There had been many times when I was desperate to do the work of writing this book and so tried disciplining myself to sit down to write, yet clarity and inspiration simply deserted me. As much as I felt the pressure of getting my thoughts onto paper in a way that is clear and concise, the words I typed were clunky, disjointed and lifeless. The problem is that producing a great book is not about working hard and just getting it done, it is about magic, inspiration, creativity and game changing ideas. To access that, I need to be in the right state.

So, right now as I am writing these very words, I'm bugging out to one of my favourite songs, which is infusing life into the core of my being. Every cell in my body is affected by what my ears are hearing. Chemistry is changing, neurology is firing, my heart is pumping, oxygen intake is increasing, ideas are sprouting, emotions are changing and the words are flowing. I have access to the outcome I desire because I am in a different state. It is my firm belief that the state you are living out of will make a world of difference to what will be possible for you.

Top sports people understand the power of state management better than most. The difference between the world's best and a player ranked in the top 100 is not actually about skill (obviously they all have incredibly high levels of skill), it's about their ability to access the magic when they need it most. An elite player may have moments of brilliance, followed by moments of madness. However, the world's best do not crumble under pressure. They are far more consistent. They can access the best of themselves under immense external pressure. If you can control your state, you can control your outcomes.

You are always in a state of some kind, but it is not always the state that will let you access the outcomes you are after. There are a whole bunch of rituals or rhythms that, when applied, will have the net result of leading you into the state that will get you the outcomes you want. Having a great state is not random. It is unlikely that you will just wake up one day 'in state'. State is crafted from inputs. If you want great outcomes you will need to learn how to get yourself into a great state. Remember, when it comes to achieving outcomes, state is king!

A Different Question

When you get up in the morning and are very clear about what you want and why you want it, instead of asking what you need *to do to* get that, ask what you need to do to get into the *right state* to get that outcome. When you are in the peak performance state for that particular outcome, the game will change. In a peak performance state you will have access to what you need to get what you really want.

More about self discipline vs self permission

Rituals are incredibly important to accessing different states. Rituals are the little things that we do all the time, whether intentionally or not, that affect our mental and emotional states. They are not connected to outcomes. Disciplines, by contrast, are actions that are directly connected to the outcome we are after. I'm convinced that most people overestimate the usefulness of discipline and underestimate the power of state. If working hard to get what you want is your best and only strategy, I guarantee the only consistent outcome you will experience is disappointment and pain.

The kinds of rituals I practice are life-giving things that create a great state. It is important to realise that rituals have a shelf life. What gives you life in one season may create a poor state in the next. I find that I need to update my rituals every nine to twelve months.

Here are some current examples of the things that are working for me:

- Morning coffee and journaling with a my magic pen and special notebook (crisp white pages with no lines)
- Dinner with friends on Sunday nights
- Golf once or twice a week

- 3 soft boiled eggs on vegemite toast with avocado and coffee for breakfast
- Thursday morning run group
- Drinking wine and eating cheese while I'm cooking dinner
- Picking the kids up from school on Friday afternoons and getting $2 of mixed lollies from the donut shop
- Popcorn and coke at the movies by myself once a fortnight
- A cold beer and plain crinkle cut chips in the bath after a tough 10-15k run
- SBS sports news at 7:15pm every night laying on my bed eating ice-cream
- Reading fiction before bed
- Watching a TV series I'm into while doing a workout on the stationary bike
- A nice arvo nap (60-90mins)
- A cup of tea with my wife while sitting in my rocking recliner, after the kids are in bed
- A drive in the country with the fam on the weekend. A travel mug with instant coffee and a choc coated muesli bar takes it to the next level!
- Sitting in my rocking chair on the front porch looking out onto the rolling hills doing creativity exercises or reading a great personal development book
- Cooking creamy porridge (like my nan makes) for the family once a week
- The 'gap loop' morning bunch ride early Friday mornings followed by coffee at the greengrocer café
- Mowing the lawn on my ride-on while listening to a podcast
- Reading the paper on a Sunday morning

I don't need to discipline myself to go to the movies once a fortnight or cook delicious porridge that reminds me of my Nan. Rather, it's about giving myself permission to do these things and go where the life is. The biggest challenge of living by state management, as opposed to just working hard through discipline and determination, is your capacity to listen to yourself and then trust yourself. Life giving rituals that create a great state are entirely subjective. What is good for me may create a really poor state in you. No one else is going to suggest I go to the movies instead of doing work, let alone give me permission to do so! Often, we are far too concerned about what we 'should' be doing and what everyone else expects of us, rather than listening to our own ideas about what would give us life and open the doors to the outcomes we want.

Every state is made up of three things:[29]

a) *Physiology*—breathing, posture, exercise
b) *Focus*—attitude, attention, energy
c) *Language*—self talk, metaphors, conversations.

Changing one or more of these can have a significant impact on our state. The rituals we practice need to be aimed at changing some or all of these things.

Morning rituals

Hal Elrod, author of 'The Miracle Morning' suggests that successful people start their day very differently than the average Joe. He attributes a big part of their success to their morning rituals that spell the acronym SAVERS:

1. *Silence*—this can be mindfulness, meditation, centredness or prayer, but the point is to stop and breathe.
2. *Affirmation*—who do you need to be to succeed? Start talking to yourself like you are that person already.
3. *Visualisation*—what results would you like? OK, go out into your future and see yourself experiencing these results so that when you get them it won't be a surprise.

4. *Exercise*—the purpose is not to gain fitness or lose weight, but to increase oxygen and blood flow to your entire body including your brain. Something short and sharp like star jumps; push-ups or a quick stair climb will do the trick.
5. *Reading*—learn something that will add value to your life. Stop reading when you've learnt one new thing for the day. This may be after one word, a paragraph, a page or a chapter.
6. *Scribing*—grab a nice pen and a clean sheet of paper and take some time to write or draw what is going on in your world.

Energy Management v's Time Management

When you become outcomes focused it is easy to become very conscious of how you are spending your time. However, effective state management is actually more about managing your energy than about managing your time. Energy is a far more useful resource that time could ever be.

Imagine you have been given a week to get an assignment done, yet you are feeling flat and totally lacking in motivation. All that time is almost useless to you. Now think of what it would be like if you only had one hour to do something important but you were in a peak state. What you could do in that hour with maximum energy is nothing short of awesome.

Who Do I Need to Be?

Once you are really clear about what you want and why you want it, the game changing question is not 'what do I need to do?' but 'who do I need to be?' Another way of asking this question is 'what kind of a person would have access to these outcomes?'

For example, let's say I want to write a book that's a best-seller. Only 2% of all authors will ever sell enough copies of their book to justify the time, money and energy they've spent in writing it. It's not simply the best books that get published, just like it's not the most talented sports person, artist or businessperson that ends up on top of the pile. Despite what most people think, the best don't always finish first. Simply doing my best isn't likely to deliver the results I am looking for. I need to find out what kind of person gets their book published and sold when most others don't. The question I need to ask myself is, "Who do I need to be to write a best-seller?"

What kind of person makes it in their field of expertise, when most work hard for very little recognition or reward? What must they believe about themselves? How do they dress? What is their relationship with money? What story do they live out of? How do they walk when they enter a room? If I can be that kind of person, then I can have access to the same results as they do. The 'be do have' model really unpacks how this works in the real world.

Be Do Have[30]

There are three common approaches to trying to get ahead in life as understood by the simple but powerful 'be do have' model. Let's call them:

- The Victim
- The Worker
- The Winner

The *victim* arranges their life in the order HAVE-DO-BE. They say, "When I HAVE enough time, money and support, then I'll DO the things I've always wanted to, and then I'll BE happy and successful. The problem is I don't HAVE yet. If I had what that person had, I'd certainly be as successful as them, but I don't so I'm not." The victim is always waiting for externals to change before they can move ahead in life.

The *worker* is all about DO-HAVE-BE.

They say, "The more I DO, the more I'll HAVE. The more I'll HAVE, the happier I'll BE. The problem is, the more I do, the more there is still to do and the more I have, the more there is still to have. I am defined by what I do so I become driven, busy and tired. The more I have, the more there is to lose so the harder I work." We all know that the link between having more things and being happier is a myth, so being happy never arrives.

The *winner* orients their life quite differently: BE-DO-HAVE. They say, "It is not what do I need to HAVE before I can start, or what work do I need to DO… but who do I need to BE? What kind of person would have access to the kind of outcomes I want? Then, being that kind of person, what would I be doing? When I get that right the 'having' takes care of itself."

BE-DO-HAVE is definitely the rarest of the three lifestyles and the most abstract, yet it is the only one that works. It really is the winner!

Self-Programming

Everyone talks to themselves, but few really pay attention to what they are saying. Successful people are very careful about what they say to themselves. You may have heard of people using positive affirmations as a strategy for living well. This strategy works, not just because the affirmations are positive, but because they help to reprogram our thinking. They help us be who we need to be to get the outcomes we desire.

Neuro Linguistic Programming (NLP) is the science of modelling excellence. Our thoughts (the neuro part) are programmed by our language (the linguistics). Shad Helmstetter in his book 'What to Say When You Are Talking to Yourself,' says that the relationship between the conscious mind and the subconscious is like that of the captain of the ship and the engine room worker.[31] The captain gives the orders (the words that he speaks) and the worker simply follows the instructions. The problem with this is that often our self-talk (the captain's orders) is quite negative and disempowering. For example, you might say to yourself: "I'm just not a very creative person…" or, "I don't make friends easily…" or, "I really suck at sports." Your subconscious hears these words as instructions and sets to work, saying, "OK great, I need to go work out how to not be a creative person…" or, "I must find a way to be terrible at making friends…" or, "It's time to be uncoordinated…" Then surprise, surprise, these are the exact results you experience, which serves to prove to you that your negative self-talk is right!

The key with self-programming is to be clear about what you really want (go back to the outcome piece) and then start talking to yourself like you are that person already. This is not simply an exercise in positive affirmations, but clear programming for the results you're looking for. It's your conscious mind giving your subconscious clear instructions to carry out.

The 'State is king' model

Let me illustrate the process of using my 'State is King' model.

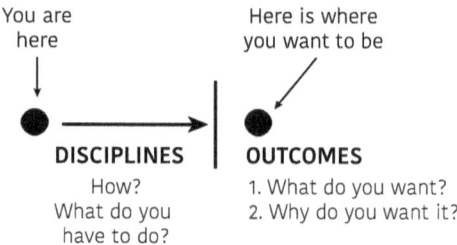

Remembering the importance of being outcomes oriented, the first question you need to ask yourself is always 'what do I want'? Then, in order to gain clarity and motivation for the desired outcome, it is essential to explore the intention behind what you want (knowing that your outcome is never about the thing you say you want, but about what that thing represents to you). So, start by asking these two key questions:

Question 1: *What do I want?*
Question 2: *Why do I want it?*

From this position the next question would typically be 'how do I get there?' Or 'what do I need to do?' You realise that where you are right now is not where you want to be and so you become desperate for a plan that is going to move you toward your desired outcome.

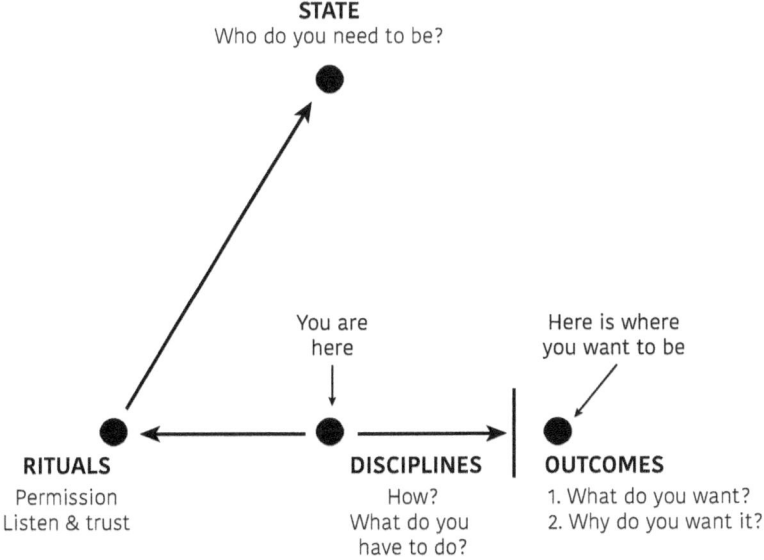

The problem is 'how?' and 'do?' are the wrong questions. It is a massive myth to believe that all that lies between you and your goals is hard work. There are plenty of people pouring blood sweat and tears into chasing their dreams and yet they are getting no closer to achieving them. It's as though there is some magical force field between them and their goal. Simply taking action and working hard towards a goal is not how successful people become successful. That road is blocked. In order to get the outcome you so desperately want, you need to take a detour and focus on something which has nothing directly to do with the outcomes you desire, but everything to do with your state.

State is the thing most responsible for outcomes. If you can control your state, you are able to control your outcomes. Some states give access to the possibility of change, while other states simply lock out those opportunities. State is king.

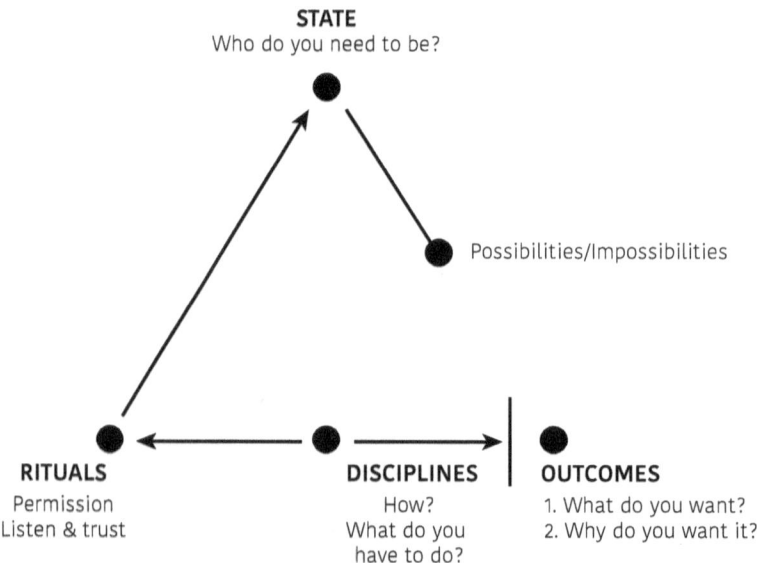

Every state has opened and closed doors. Each state comes pre-loaded with possibilities and impossibilities. In one state motivation, creativity, passion and energy will be possible and you can readily access these things as much as you need, while in a different state, it's as though the door has been locked to these things and no matter how hard you try, they will be impossible to access.

It turns out that the outcomes we are able to achieve in any given moment are simply the fruit of the possibilities we have access to, based on the state that we are in.

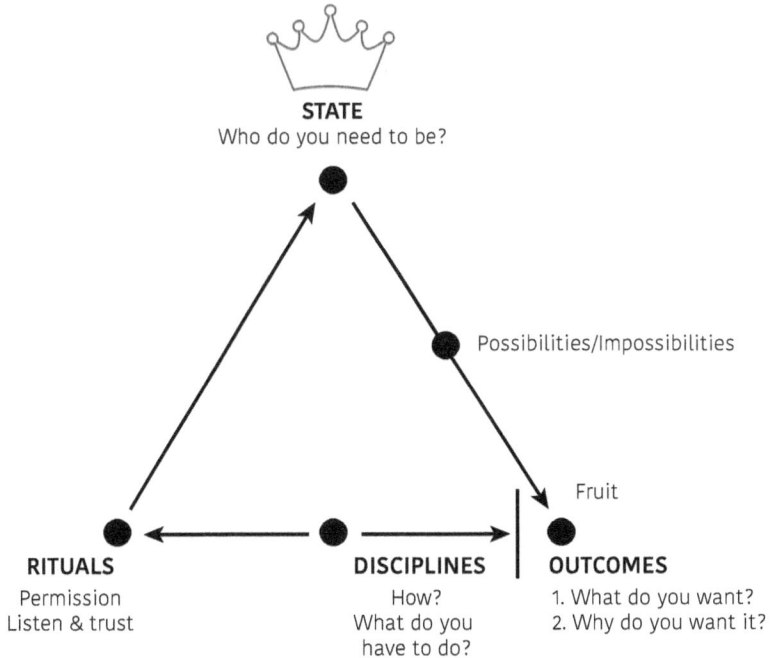

When we realise this, our attention goes back to the things that affect our state, namely rituals and anchors.

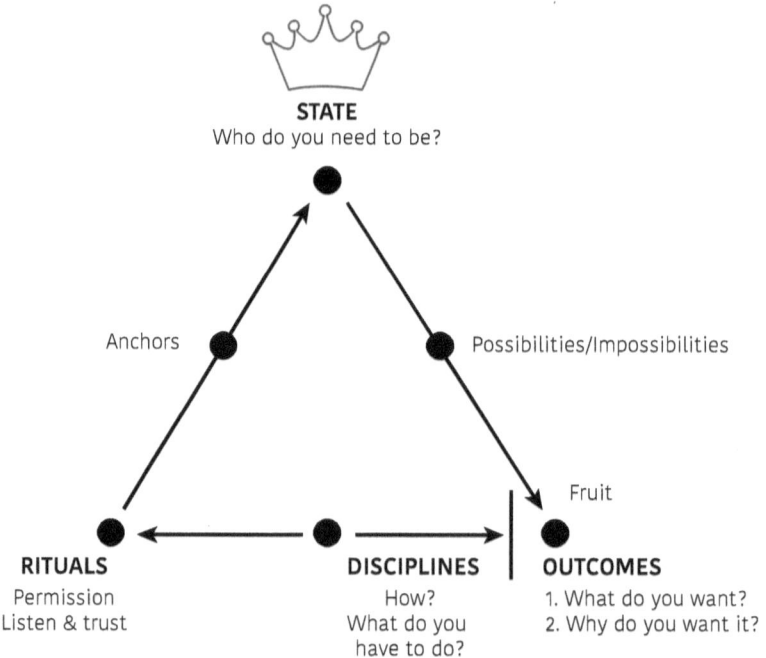

State is such a remarkable thing. It can change almost instantly in response to the minutest stimulus. We can go from having no motivation, energy, clarity or confidence one minute, to being almost the opposite moments later. For example, think of the times when you have gone from tired to inspired when your partner shows desire, or from flat to excited when a friend calls with good news.

When it comes to managing state, rituals—the little things we do that affect our state—become very important. Disciplines—the hard work activities that have a direct link to our desired outcomes—on their own, are not enough.

Anchors are another important key to effective state management. Anchors are subconscious links between a state of being and a sensual trigger. We naturally anchor sights, smells, feelings, sounds etc. with certain events, times or emotions.

For example, we may experience a feeling of being loved simply by smelling the perfume our mother wore. In NLP, the term "anchoring" refers to the process of associating an internal response with some external or internal trigger so that the response may be quickly, and sometimes covertly, re-accessed. On the surface the process is similar to the "conditioning" technique used by Pavlov to create a link between the hearing of a bell and salivation in dogs. By associating the sound of a bell with the act of giving food to his dogs, Pavlov found he could eventually just ring the bell and the dogs would start salivating, even though no food was given.[32] Anchors are very useful for helping to quickly access key peak performance states.

Here is the flow of ideas for how this model hits the ground:

1. What do I want?
2. Why do I want it?
3. Who would I need to be to get access to those kind of results?
4. What state would open these doors?
5. What rituals would create that kind of state?

Life Lessons in State Management

My three day experience with my mentor started and ended with object lessons about state management that I will never forget.

Lesson One

On our trip up the coast toward our camping spot, Ian invited me to give him a picture of what was happening in my world. Five minutes into the conversation he pulled me up, noticing that I appeared to be embarrassed about some of the stuff I was sharing. He questioned the intention behind my embarrassed state and asked me what my overall desired outcome was for the twelve months of mentoring with him (after all, I'd paid a lot of money for the privilege). I shared with him my honest desire to become the best coach in the country and my desperation to learn everything possible from someone who was clearly leading the pack.

"Ok great," he replied, "so how is being in a state of embarrassment giving you access to that outcome?" He paused while I pondered the question.

"What state would you need to be in to maximise your learning experience right now? How would you be sitting? How would you be feeling in your body? What would you be focused on?" Another pause. "Have you got it?" I nodded. "OK great, now start again so you can experience this conversation from a very different state." So I did just that and my experience of the conversation changed dramatically.

Lesson Two

About a month before the camping trip, Ian had asked me if I'd ever been rock climbing before. "Yeah for sure," I had replied, thinking of the five metre high indoor climbing wall at the local PCYC. When we arrived at the campsite, I quickly discovered that he had something very different in mind. Our first climb was a 60 metre limestone beach cliff face. He gave me a run through how the rope system worked and what I needed to do, and then he was off. As I watched him scale the face with ease, I eagerly anticipated my turn, very confident that despite being on the edge of my comfort zone, I'd smash it!

I started out beautifully. About half way up I got stuck. It didn't take long for panic to set in. My body started to freeze up. I remember questioning the rationale behind my subconscious sending an abundance of liquid to the skin of my hands at a time when my life depended on high-quality grip. I glanced down at the waves crashing into the wall below, then looked way up to where

Ian was perched, waiting for me. I felt completely vulnerable and afraid.

After failing to find any viable way out of the situation, I yelled out to Ian that I was about to fall. He hollered back, "What do you mean? Just lean back on the rope!" Against my natural instinct, I pried my fingers off the cliff face and grasped the rope, gradually letting it take my weight. This gave me the freedom to walk sideways across the rock and find a better hold and a new path to the top. In literally 30 seconds, my state changed from white-knuckled panic to being so relaxed and at ease in my surroundings that I could have gone to sleep. Every cell in my body was now enjoying a very different experience, simply because my focus had changed. One minute I was focused on my height above the crashing waves below, and not being able to find my next hold. After listening to Ian's instruction, I was now focused entirely on the rope, knowing that the worst case scenario, should I slip, was a drop of no more than 30 centimetres. I was completely safe and free to play.

My well-formed outcome was to get to the top of the cliff without dying (and keeping my underpants clean). My first state had no access to that outcome. My second state made it simple.

Lesson Three

On the final evening of the trip we were enjoying a glass of wine while watching the sun go down. I finally plucked up the courage to bring the biggest issue of my life to the table. Twenty seconds into my story, Ian noticed my state and immediately interrupted.

"You're embarrassed again aren't you?"

"Ha ha... Yeah, I am a bit," I said, now really embarrassed.

"Well stop f#%ing wasting my time!" And with that, he got up and walked off.

I *so* got the point…I mean; it's a judgment free space. He couldn't care less about what was going on in my world that I felt bad about.

I had clearly stated my desired outcomes for the trip, and then I'd just shown up to a key conversation in a state that was locking me out of what I said I wanted.

What's the point of that?!

That trip deeply embedded in me the significance of these two most important questions:

Question 1: *What do I want (stated as specifically as possible)?*
Question 2: *What state do I need to be in to have access to that outcome?*

Everything else is a waste of time.

Managing State for Outcomes

When I say that state is king, some people hear me say 'King' state is king. What I actually mean is that the state we are in is the most accurate predictor of the results we should expect. Different desired outcomes will require completely different states and not all of those will be high performance (King) states. Have a look at these outcomes and consider what states they require:

- Eight hours of great sleep
- Being a present father to my kids after work
- Delivering a presentation to a group
- Having a fun day off work
- Running a 10km time trial
- Coaching a client
- Taking my wife on a date
- Rock climbing 60m cliff face
- Having dinner with friends

- Singing karaoke with my mates

Each one of those outcomes require me to access very different internal resources. It's crazy and totally unrealistic to try and live out of a peak state all the time and expect to get the outcomes you are looking for. The key issue is whether you have sufficient access points (e.g. rituals, anchors, choice around physiology, psychology and biochemistry) to access the states you need when you need them.

I have a Parramatta Eels football jumper that is anchored to being in a very earthy, relaxed, agricultural state. When I need to fix the mower, cut fire wood, help a mate move house, have a bonfire with the lads, or go bushwalking I put that jumper on and bingo… I have access to my desired state. When I want to be creative, it's the booth at the Park Café. When I want to be confident, it's my favourite cologne and special jacket. When I want connection, friendship and laughter, it is the bench at the Greengrocer Café. When I want to unwind, it's a cup of tea in my rocking chair.

Once, when I was doing a group coaching session with a business team, I gave the owner of the business a chance to speak to his staff during the session. He had some great things to say and his content was really well thought out, however, two minutes into his presentation I noticed one of the team leaders reach his left arm across his chest and start rubbing the side of his neck. He continued to do this for the next ten minutes while his boss spoke.

It was very clear that this guy was in a state of shutdown and self-protection. His eyes were glazed over and he was not hearing a word that was being said. His arm across his chest, as if to protect his vital organs, suggested he was feeling threatened and under attack. Rubbing his neck suggested he was feeling stressed and anxious. Unfortunately, the owner failed to notice and missed the opportunity to manage the state of his team. As a result, his attempt at stirring motivation and passion was entirely counter-productive.

There's no point pushing on in a conversation when those we are trying to communicate with are in a state of fear, boredom, anxiety or frustration. State is king. Every state has opened and closed doors. The state we are in determines what is possible and impossible. When we fail to pay attention to state we can't manage it. When we don't manage state effectively we don't have access to the outcomes we are looking for.

Questions

- *How often do you use a 'discipline' approach rather than a 'permission' approach to get your desired outcomes?*

- *What gives you life? What is good for your soul?*

- *How well do currently manage your state? How well do you match your state to the task at hand?*

- *What would happen if you paid more attention to getting into the right state rather than fighting through your to-do-list as your first priority?*

- *Have you experienced the sense of doors opening and closing based on the state you're in?*

- *What would you like to have happen?*

- *Have you developed that into a clear, well defined outcome?*

- *What state would you need to be in to give you access to that outcome?*

So, that's the sixth and final piece in the coaching frame. I am trusting that you now have a clear understanding of the nature of the coaching relationship and the frame through which we are exploring the content in the remainder of this book. Take a moment to check in and make sure you are experiencing a state which makes change possible. If you are not, I would highly recommend you find a way to access that state before your proceed.

Part Two

A MODEL FOR CHANGE

INTRODUCTION

People often imagine that their problems are incredibly complicated and totally unique, the beautiful thing is that they are neither. While the solutions may not be easy, they are never complicated. And we all go through the same kinds of challenges in different ways, so our issues are never uniquely ours to solve and we are never alone in our struggle. The way forward is always simple and hard.

Now that you understand the coaching frame and are in a great state for getting the change outcomes you are after, let's take a look at the elegantly simple solutions to our complicated people problems.

In the following chapters I'll describe the basic symptoms or problems people commonly face. For each of these symptoms I will show you the cause, outline the solution and identify the fruit we are looking for. So let's get started.

Let me explain how this works, one piece of the puzzle at a time…

Chapter Seven

HOPELESSNESS

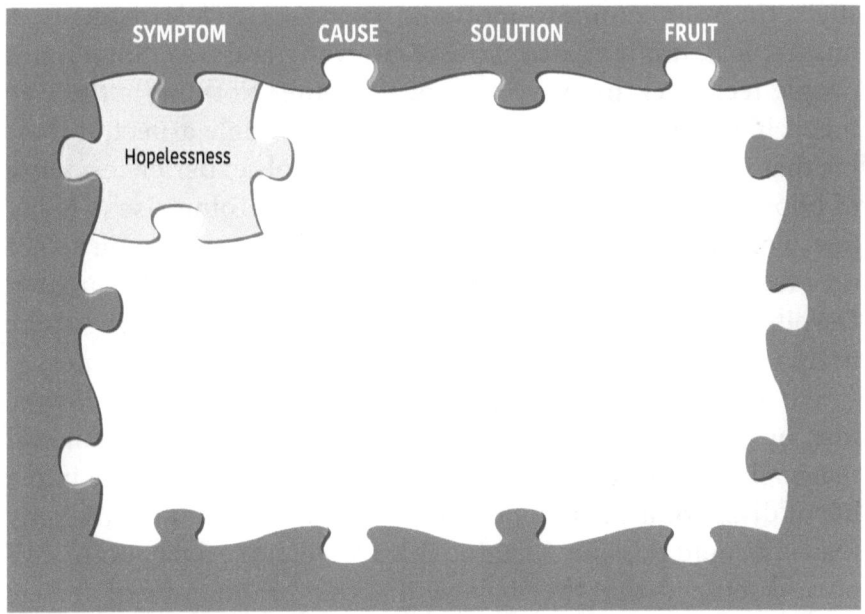

T HE FIRST OF THE 3 MAIN SYMPTOMS PEOPLE COMMONLY experience in life is hopelessness. It is what happens when you feel stuck and when you have no idea how to change the painful stuff in your life.

Symptom 1: Hopelessness

When people find themselves in situations that are not how they'd like them to be, they experience the sense of hopelessness. This words sums up the feeling of being stuck, limited, trapped or really unsure about what to do to change things. Even though you've tried everything you can think of, nothing has resolved the issue and now you really have no idea how to fix it. You may even wonder if there is a next move at all. Every 'complicated' and 'unique' people problem includes elements of hopelessness.

Studies show that there is a link between making progress and feeling a sense of happiness.[33] When it appears that we've become stuck, the most common emotional response is to feel dissatisfied, unsure, lost, unmotivated, limited or even paralysed. Sometimes people feel stuck in every area of their life. Nothing is the way they'd like it to be and they can't point to a single aspect of their life that is moving forward. More often, people experience a sense of hopelessness in one or two areas and everything else is going fine. For example, work and heath may be great, but you've got no idea how to connect with your fourteen year old daughter. Despite the success in other areas, the experience of being stuck in this one area has the power to create a sense of hopelessness.

Often people cope with feeling stuck by pretending that they're fine, or by imagining that if they just ignore the situation it will magically resolve itself. In the end they give up. They settle into a life of disappointment, depression, fatigue or addiction. The only reason I could possibly imagine that would cause a person to give up and settle, is that they believe that there is no hope of change or improvement in their life. The aim of this model is to show you there is always a solution to this problem.

Hopelessness affects us all differently. Some people give up more quickly than others. Yet it still never ceases to amaze me how resilient people are in their ability to keep surviving in situations that they hate and feel hopeless about.

For the first few years of my coaching experience, my most common client was a middle aged woman whose kids have grown up and left home. She has woken up one morning feeling incredibly lost. She has no clear sense of purpose anymore and on top of this, she realises that she doesn't like (let alone love) her husband anymore. All she has known for the last 30 years has been the parenting role, which she has invested herself into whole-heartedly.

While I acknowledge that men certainly have lots of common challenges in life, I believe a woman's greatest challenge is not losing herself in the word 'mother'. So often a mum takes on the suffering servant role in the home and seems to exist for everyone else's happiness. This role defines who she is. Her whole value, worth and identity as a person gets tied up in this function. It's no wonder then that when the kiddies grow up and leave home, she feels lost and disconnected from her husband. Before she was mother, she was wife and before that she was her own woman. Unfortunately, the woman she really is has been lost behind years of attachment to the role she has been playing. She now feels stuck and ill equipped to move forward. It all feels so complicated… I mean where can she even begin?

Another common client is someone who has been without a job for some length of time. They know they're supposed to get a job and they really want to, but it all seems so daunting and difficult. The modern world of technology is so complicated and fast paced. They are so far behind compared to the kids graduating from high school. It just seems impossible. If only they had applied themselves at school or not lost their license due to a DUI infringement… If only their parents had encouraged them to go to Uni, or their girlfriend hadn't run off with all their money… If only (insert story here…)

Or maybe its marriage troubles, work issues, constant sickness, broken friendships, personal challenges, the struggle to lose weight, overcoming fears, running a small business, dealing with the in-laws… the list goes on. People try all that they know and then find they don't know what else to do. Change seems like such a long way off. The anxiety, the stress, the struggle to sleep at night tells them that it all seems hopeless.

You may be reading this thinking that there are no areas of hopelessness in your life. While this may in fact be the case, perhaps, in moments of real honesty, you can see that there are some areas of life that are not how you really want them to be and you don't know how to fix them. Facing this truth it is really painful, so you avoid it as a way of getting by and feeling OK about your life.

Maybe 'hopeless' doesn't quite describe your condition, but whatever the word, whatever the stat you want something to change but have no idea how to change it.

Questions

- *Where in your life do you appear to be stuck, trapped or limited?*

- *Are there issues you have made numerous attempts to change, yet nothing has worked?*

- *If you were really honest with how you feel about your situation (rather than pretending you are fine) how would you describe the emotions associated with being stuck?*

- *If a favourable way out of your current situation existed, would you take it?*

Chapter Eight

THE ILLUSION OF NO CHOICE

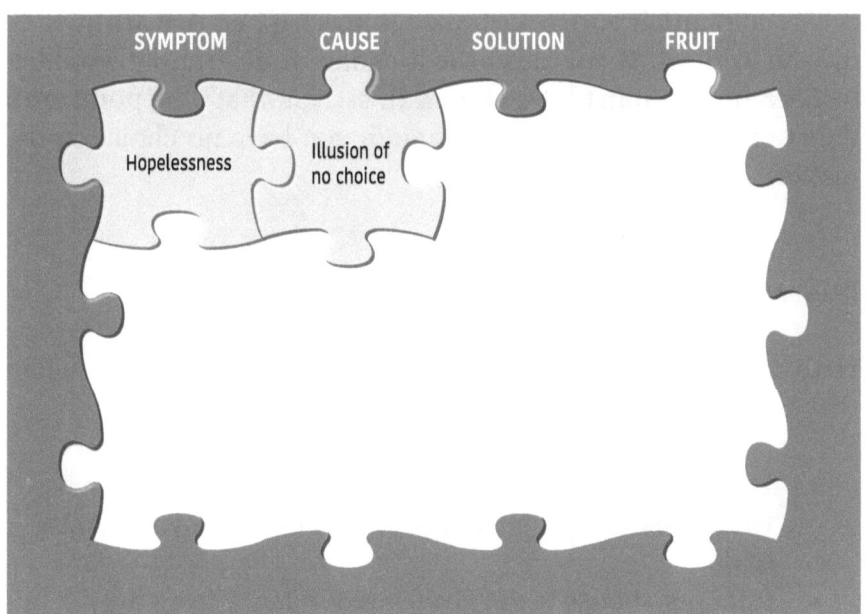

T̲he root cause of 'hopelessness' is living with the illusion of no choice and feeling as though you are out of options. You have done everything you know to do and nothing has worked.

Cause 1: The illusion of no choice

If you've got five options and four of them expire, then there is still hope. But if all your perceived options run out, then hope evaporates immediately. The feelings of hopelessness are ultimately not about self-esteem, success, happiness, progress, significance, love or anything else. The root of the problem is feeling like you have no choice and that you are out of believable alternatives.

If you are in the midst of hopelessness, the real problem is the feeling that you have found yourself in a place that you did NOT choose. You believe you are here because of other people's choices that have affected you detrimentally. It's really not your fault. Life is hard and unfair and unfortunate things happen that are outside of your control. If you did have a choice you certainly wouldn't be here and wouldn't have chosen this… but that's the point. You didn't choose this. You feel as though you have no choice in the matter.

It is what it is…

Here are some great examples of what people experience when they believe they have no choice:

- I did not choose to be unemployed and everything I have tried to fix this problem has failed. I don't know what else to do.
- I did not choose to get given a redundancy from my job of 20 years. It's the only work I've ever done. I have no other qualifications or experience, and there are no other jobs available in this field.
- I did not choose for my husband to have an affair. I've passed my prime and couldn't imagine being 'on the market' again. Now he's made me be alone for the rest of my life.

- I did not choose to be born this way. My physical disability totally limits my options in life.
- I did not choose for my kids to treat me poorly and take my grand kids overseas so I don't get to see them anymore. I have no money to travel so I guess I'll never see them.
- I did not choose to have a drunk driver crash into my car and leave me permanently injured. It is impossible to be happy when I have lost so much.
- I did not choose to be abused. What happened to me has left me unable to trust anyone or be intimate.

Once we resign ourselves to the fact that we are stuck (or hopeless, or whatever other word you want to use to describe this condition) we often resort to a strategy of sharing our story so others will understand our situation and give us sympathy or pity. Our only hope is that if others could just understand what terrible things have happened, they wont judge us for being here! When we are living with the illusion of no choice our stories are characterised by words such as 'have to, need to, must or should.' These words convey a sense of obligation because they remove choice from the equation. The use of these words alone can cause us to feel stuck, trapped or limited unable to break out of the program we feel locked into. The words we use don't just describe our experience they actually shape them. Using the common phrase "It is what it is" further embeds you in the cycle of 'stuckness'.

The surprising truth

It is entirely impossible to be out of options and have no choice, even when it appears that way. Having no choice is merely an illusion. If we lift the curtain up, we will discover that in actual fact we have 100% choice. While we may not choose what happens to us, we always get to choose our response. We get to choose everything that matters in determining the quality of our lives.

This is a crucial piece in the puzzle. While ever you believe you have no choice, you will get stuck and find areas of hopelessness in your life

Questions

- *Where in your life are you living with the illusion of no choice?*

- *In what areas of life do you use words like should, have to, must, need to?*

- *Where do you feel other people's choices have really taken away your own sense of choice?*

Chapter Nine

EMBRACING 100% CHOICE

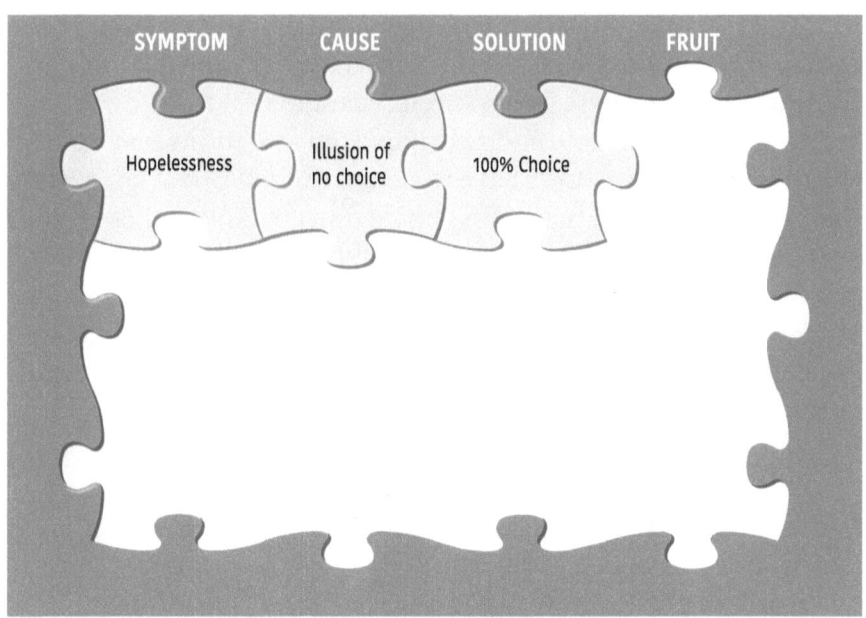

People feel stuck, because they are living with the illusion of no choice. The way out of 'stuckness' is found seeing through the illusion and becoming aware of an abundance of real choice.

Solution 1: Embracing 100% choice

The way out of 'hopelessness' is to embrace 100% choice. As confronting and offensive as it sounds, we are all exactly where we have chosen to be. Sure, there are always things that happen to us that we did not and would not choose, but we always get to choose our response. That is firmly in our domain and no one has the power to take that from us.

When we operate with the illusion of no choice we get stuck in situations of obligation where it seems like the only option is to do what we have to do rather than what we want to do; "I have to go to work...I need to visit my parents...I have to provide for my family...I must finish my Uni degree...I should exercise...I have to do what my boss wants." This language robs us of power and positions us as victims to our circumstances.

However immovable and restrictive our situations may appear, the reality is that we don't have to do anything. I'm not suggesting that it is a good idea, but some people don't do any of these things and get away with it! When we live out of obligation everything is done grudgingly with a growing sense of resentment. This kind of living always leaves people feeling unhappy, stuck and hopeless. Empowered living, on the other hand, always begins with embracing 100% choice.

We are Exactly Where We've Chosen to Be

I had the opportunity to work with a man in his 50's who had been struggling with depression for over 30 years. He had been referred to me by a family member as a last ditch effort to help him get out of the dark place he'd been living in for most of his adult life. I can still remember the stunned look on his face when I hit him with my first question, "Tell me, how is this depression NOT a problem for you?" He tried hard to escape the question, by telling me as much as possible about how depression WAS a problem. I held the space and waited for him to face it. His only way of understanding his depression was to see it as some horrible external affliction that had come on him from somewhere outside, and that all he could possibly do was medicate it and develop coping mechanisms to survive.

This one question caused him to face this illusion of no choice he was living with. As he processed my question he gradually began to admit that having depression had its hidden rewards. The moment he felt unsure, insecure, overwhelmed or uncertain about how to deal with the challenges of life, he could pull out his magical 'get out of jail free' depression card. This allowed him to escape and hide behind his depression for as long as he liked, as often as he liked, every time. No one could question him or hold him accountable, because he had a valid excuse!

Now, I'm not saying that depression is not a thing. It's definitely a real thing, but so often people feel that the things that are causing them most grief in life are holding onto them, when in reality they are the ones doing the holding on.

Whatever chemistry, biology and physiology is happening for this guy, ultimately he was still the one choosing to be depressed. Remember, every single thing that we tolerate or complain about but do not change MUST be giving us a payoff. Otherwise we would have moved on already. Human psychology 101.

See this is a game changing moment in this apparently complex and unique problem. If he is in fact choosing the depression, as confronting and offensive as that is, nothing changes until he chooses to be free.

I always remember reading about Viktor Frankl in Stephen Covey's book 'The 7 Habits of Highly Effective People.' Despite the fact that this man had lost every earthly possession, everyone he loved had been killed and he was living in hell on earth in a Nazi death camp, he did not lose hope because he embraced the power of choice. His story deserves retelling again and again.

"One day, naked and alone in a small room, he began to become aware of what he later called 'the last of human freedoms'—the freedom his Nazi captors could not take away. They could control his entire environment, they could do what they wanted to his body, but Viktor Frankl himself was a self-aware being who could look as an observer at his very involvement. His basic identity was intact. He could decide within himself how this was going to affect him. Between what happened to him, or the stimulus and his response to it, was his freedom or power to choose that response."[34]

There are so many amazing and powerful things we get to choose in life. Here are a few of them:

We Get to Choose Our Response

Because we have the ability to use imagination, self-awareness, conscience and independent will, we always have the freedom to choose our response, no matter what the stimulus in front of us. No one has the power to make us happy, sad, angry or excited. We get to choose how we respond, what we think about the situation and how we feel.

We have real choice. High stakes choice. There are no guarantees in life, that's what makes it so incredible. God's greatest and most loving gift to us is real choice. It's easier to pretend that fate controls everything of course, because then we have no choice, and nothing is our fault. Choice means our lives are real. Imagine if we were robots completely programmed and controlled by someone else. Although this may eliminate the horrible things people do with their free will, it would also eliminate the beautiful things. The fact that we actually have the ability to make real choices and we are not just living out of a script means that life is not just a game with a predetermined outcome that we cannot control. This thing is real!

We can do incredible things with our choices and also horrible things. We can just as easily bring life, love and blessing to others as we can death, pain and suffering. All the things we value most about life are only real because we have choice. How can you say you've done a good thing unless there you had the choice to do the alternative? Good, without bad, is meaningless. Would love mean anything at all if you had to (were forced to) love? The very thing that makes love so wonderful is that you don't have to give it… you choose to.

The amazing thing is that when we begin to scratch the surface, it is extraordinary how much choice we really have. We get to choose everything that matters.

We Get to Choose What Things Mean

Whether you realise it or not, you have had the privilege of choosing the meaning of every event, conversation and experience you have faced in life from the moment you were born. Your experience of life is not based what happens to you; rather it is shaped by the meaning you place on these things. I get to work with plenty of people who have experienced some form of abuse in their childhood. Typically they believe their life is so messed up today because of what was done to them in the past. Yet incredibly, the abuse is not the thing that ruined their life (as horrible as that was). The real damage was caused by what they told themselves about why they were abused and what that means about them. This story they have told themselves is what has created the major problems in their life.

Even though we imagine that the stuff that happens in life comes with an attached meaning, it turns out that nothing has meaning attached except the meaning we give it. In order to see lasting change in your life, at some point it is essential to accept that all we have is story. We are sense-making creatures who go into the world and tell stories to give meaning to our experiences. It's all just story! There are a multitude of stories that could be told about every experience we have. Each story leads to a very different destination, and the quality of our life is largely determined by the quality of the stories we tell.

The key is to own the fact that you are the one choosing your story. It is not being chosen for you. You are not just an actor in the story, but you are the story-teller. If you don't like the stories you have told about your life to this point, you and only you can go back and write new ones.

Just because someone says something mean, cruel or belittling to you doesn't shape your life. That is living under the illusion of no choice. You are the one who decides if what they said is true or not. You are the one who decides why they said it. And you are the one who cannot help making choices about what this means about you and how this will affect your future. It's all you!

If life was simply about what happens to each of us, then if you've had bad things happen to you, you will have a bad life or if you've had good things happen to you, you will have a good life!

Obviously this is not how the world works though. I'm sure we all know people who have been through horrific and unfair situations in life yet have gone onto to do amazing things, and others who've had everything handed to them and yet not really done anything noteworthy with their life!

If two people were to have a conversation with whom does the meaning of that conversation reside after they have gone their separate ways? Both parties often walk away with very different stories about what was just transacted. It doesn't matter what the speaker intended or thought they were saying, the only thing that matters is how the listener interpreted what was said. This is what makes great communication so challenging!

The same is true in every event in our lives. We each choose the meaning of each event based on what we perceive to have taken place. Once we form meaning, we develop feelings of certainty about that meaning and become convinced they are true. The meaning we give to our experiences form the basis of our beliefs. Our beliefs then become our filtering system for life and become self-fulfilling prophecies for our future.

The NLP communication model

Originally conceived and developed by John Grinder and Richard Bandler, the NLP Communication Model[35] explains how we process the abundance of information our senses have access to in any one moment. According to this model, when we experience an external event we run that event through the filter of our internal processing. This filter is made up of our beliefs, attitudes, memories, values, language and programming. We then make an internal representation of that event which helps us make sense of it. We gather evidence to support what we believe while simultaneously deleting, distorting or generalising all other evidence.

Bandler and Grinder estimated that every second of the day, our senses are processing at least two million bits of information. We only have the capacity to be consciously present to around seven bits of that information each second, so the rest gets filtered out and rendered irrelevant or unimportant. It is amazing to discover that we filter out the vast majority of information that is available to us in any given moment.

When in doubt about meaning, it seems that we tend towards picking a negative meaning about ourselves—especially as children. The meaning we choose then forms a limiting belief, which creates a self-perpetuating story about our own inadequacy. This belief goes on generating more and more evidence until we are convinced it is the truth.

We Get to Choose our Beliefs

So, as it turns out, when we choose a meaning, we are also setting ourselves up to choose a *belief*. The incredible thing is that these beliefs act as a filter, deleting, distorting or generalising all the information we are constantly bombarded with, so that we are only delivered the evidence that proves the belief is true. Our beliefs, meanings and stories are all powerful works of fiction that shape our experience of reality. Fortunately, it is possible to reshape these beliefs. Fortunately, it is possible to reshape these beliefs. Here are three steps in seeing long-held, limiting beliefs changed.

A) Defining moments.

In order to change a belief and untangle the painful stories of lack, limitation and insecurity, it is essential to go back to the place the belief was first created and then exercise the power of 100% choice.

Most people try and deal with the mess in their heads by pretending it doesn't exist or through self-medication and various coping strategies. It often feels too painful and overwhelming to try and untangle the mess and get to the bottom of it.

Yet, if you don't find a way to change the belief, your only alternative is to manage the behaviour that belief constantly produces. Without going back to where that limiting story was first created means you are always managing mess inside your head and heart that is stopping you being at your best.

Here are a few key ideas to help you do the real work of untangling your stories today.

1. Become aware of the story. What is the story you are living out of and what kind of character are you in that story? A great way to do this is simply to observe your patterns of behaviour, (behaviour never lies. It always flows out of our beliefs.) Then ask 'what MUST I believe in order to behave this way?'
2. Become aware of the beginning of that belief. When was the first time you told yourself this was true? Who else had a part in writing this story with you? While you may not have conscious awareness of the answer to the origin question, subconsciously the answer is always there. If the two parts

of our brain were like a computer, the conscious has about 4 gig on the hard drive (enough room for some songs, pics and videos) while the subconscious has terabytes of storage! Everything you have ever seen, heard and experienced is all stored there somewhere. Obviously you don't have room in your conscious for every memory, but they are all there deep beneath the surface. If you are ready and willing, you can gain access to the key defining moments where limiting beliefs first entered into your world.
3. The key is not only to be aware of what happened to you, but the meaning you placed on these events. What did you decide it meant about you?

B) The gift of doubt

1. Accept that all we have is story. We are sense-making creatures who go into the world and tell stories to give meaning to our experiences. It's all just a story though. It's all a work of fiction. - There are a multitude of other stories that could be told about the same experience. Each story leads to a very different destination.
2. What else could be true? The aim is not to find the "true" meaning. How could you possibly know what is true? Exercising 100% choice is simply about choosing stories that work for you. If it doesn't get you more of what you want, well pick a different meaning until it does. What else could the key moments in your life mean?

C) Create empowering beliefs.

1. Realise there was a time in your life before this story was true for you. That means the story you are living out of is not you. It is an addition to your life, it is not who you are.
2. Take responsibility for the fact that you are not just an actor in the story, but you are the storyteller. If you don't like the

stories you have told about your life to this point, you and only you can go back and write new ones.
3. What would you need to believe to get more of what you want? How would you know the new belief is any less true than the limiting one you've held onto all these years and have a mountain of evidence for?

Now it just becomes a matter of choosing between two equally fictitious beliefs:
Which one is going to work better for you and those you care about?
Which one will be more fun?
Which one will get you the kind of results you are looking for? (Handy hint... pick that one!)

Change becomes possible when we realise we are living out of a story. Remember, the story we tell ourselves about our lives is based on the meanings we have chosen and the beliefs we have formed based on those meanings. Our story seems to be 100% true, and we've spent years collecting evidence to prove to ourselves that it is. Whatever we believe, we find evidence for. It's just a story. People who succeed in life do so largely on the back of the stories they tell themselves.

This process it not easy, but neither is it complicated.

What would I need to believe?

A few years before I started my own coaching business, I worked as a school chaplain in one of our local high schools. When I saw the job advertised, I immediately thought it would be something I'd love to pursue. However, I was aware that one of my friends, who was working in the school as a casual teacher, also had his eye on the job and had been waiting for it to become available. I gave him a call to see how he felt about me putting my application forward. The last thing I wanted to do was tread on his toes or ruin his plans. I was surprised to discover that he was totally relaxed about me applying. "That's fine," he said, "I'll get the job, but if you'd like to have a crack at it, go for your life." He clearly had different beliefs than I did, both about the job and the capacity we each had to land it. A week later I had the job.

The school had never had a chaplain before and I can still remember the principal walking me around the school giving me my job description. "You are not a parent, nor a teacher… you are a chaplain. You're on the kid's team. Your job is to make friends with all 800 of them. Look after them, love them, support them and just be there for them. Got it?"

I was slightly alarmed if not a little overwhelmed. My beliefs told me that you can't just bound up to a teenager and make friends with them. Half the kids were way too cool for school and would probably beat me up and steal my sneakers if I so much as looked at them wrong. When I was a student at school it was tough to make friends. I didn't have many of them, and the ones I did have took lots of hard work. My beliefs told me that, as the new school chaplain, the safest thing would be to hide in my office and wait for the needy kids to come and find me. And yet I'd just been given a brief that told me I had to get out there and become Mr. Popular.

I really wanted to be a great school chaplain and make the most of this opportunity to make a significant difference in the school. As I stood there, I realised that in order to be effective in my role, I'd need to believe that everyone in the school liked me… and why wouldn't they? My challenge was that I actually believed the opposite and this stood in direct opposition to my desired outcome. While my old belief felt true, in reality it was just a story. At the same time, the new belief was not true either. In that moment I had a choice between two equally untrue beliefs. Ultimately, the decision came down to which belief would be more fun and would get me more of what I wanted.

Every day for the first six weeks I literally had to put the new belief on like a jumper every time I arrived at the school. It didn't come naturally and it wasn't easy, yet very soon, I started gathering evidence for this new belief. Two years later, when I announced at the school assembly that I was leaving the job to start my own coaching company, I got a standing ovation from every student in the school. Wow... the power of a changed belief. I certainly wouldn't have got that result with my old belief.

Because we have 100% choice, we are in control. We are not victims of our world. Even when we have made choices that have hurt us or others, every passing moment provides another chance to turn it all around. We get a fresh opportunity to discover more choice, new choice and better choice.

We Get to Choose Our State

I'm sure you've experienced the highs of being in an incredible state when life is grand and the lows of being in a horrible state when things are going badly. Yet, as we explored in chapter six, state is firmly in our domain no matter what is going on around us. Our mental, emotional and physical state is deeply affected by things firmly within our control.

We are constantly making choices about:

- The language we use;
- The things we are focused on; and
- What we do with our physiology.

To get a sense of what I mean, simply take a moment to notice what you are focused on right now. What else could you be focused on? Check the kind of language you're using in your self-talk and in the way you are talking to those around you. What other kind of words could you be using? Observe what is happening in your body. How are you sitting or standing? How quickly and deeply are you breathing? What kind of clothes are you wearing? What's happening with your hair-do? What else could you do with your body? Every adjustment you make with focus, language and physiology also completely changes your state.

Let me show you more about the choices we have within each of these three state-affecting areas of life.

We Get to Choose the Language We Use

The words we use don't just describe how we feel, they also shape our experience of reality. If you change the words you use, you also change the experience you have of what you are describing. It's another way to change the frame. If you say you hate something or someone, the word 'hate' will generate a very strong emotional response. If that state serves you, great, keep the word, but if that's not the state you would like to be in, pick a different word and watch your emotional response change with it.

When a person is really stuck in 'hopelessness' and quite afraid at the thought of venturing forward, I ask them to promise me that they will not change anything about their life after our first session. They must guarantee that they will not deal with any of their doubts, fears or limiting beliefs or step outside their comfort zone. Having made this solemn vow, I ask them if they would be willing to just play with one word as a way of dipping their toe into the waters of change. Every time they go to use the word 'can't' I invite them to replace it with the honest version of what they are really saying, which is, 'I've chosen not to.' Typically, a person who feels hopeless about something will use the word 'can't' frequently. "I can't change…" or, "I can't lose weight…" or, "I can't understand my teenage son…" or, "I can't restore my marriage…" or, "I can't get a job…" or, "I can't make friends…" or, "I can't get a promotion…" or, "I can't manage my money."

All I ask of my clients is that they eliminate the word 'can't' and simply say, "I've chosen not to (insert story here)." Initially, this sounds like it couldn't be true. Of course they want these things, so it couldn't be their choice not to have them. But the truth is, some part of them doesn't really want it. The moment we truly want something, we will find a way to go after it and, the vast majority of the time, we will create a way to experience what we are looking for.

This exercise is all about sitting with the reality of the choices we each make every day. Every single thing we complain about but don't change must be working for us or giving us some kind of pay off. As good old Dr. Phil says, "We are not that stupid to do things for zero reward." More often than not, the next time I see them they are begging me to let them change some stuff that they were terrified to change the week before, simply because they are beginning to see that they have far more choice than they ever imagined.

The questions we ask ourselves fit under the heading of the language we are choosing. It's totally understandable for someone just diagnosed with cancer to ask 'why me?' But that's not the only question they could ask. While 'why me?' is a reasonable question to jump to, there is frequently no useful answer to that question, and its effect on their state is terrible. Nick Vujicic, an Aussie guy born without any arms and legs, had every reason to ask that question (and probably did for much of his childhood). His life took a profound turn when he found a more useful question. In a moment of curiosity he asked, "How can I use this to get more of what I want?" This question immediately changed how he experienced his physical condition. One minute it was a massive and unfair limitation that caused him to want to end his life. The next it was an unfair advantage that was his doorway to international influence. Choosing to be ignorant about the conscious and unconscious power of your words can have serious consequences. If you want better outcomes, own the fact that you get to choose your language and pick words that create the kind of experience you want to have.

The metaphors we use in our daily conversations (with ourselves and others) are another key aspect of our choices around language. Metaphors are the bridge between the conscious and the subconscious and we use them to link the known to the unknown. They take something our brain knows and understands and sticks it with something hard to grasp or explain.

Metaphors affect so much about our lives without us even realising. They form the structure to our experience and frame what we expect to happen. Here is an example: There is something important you have to get done, when someone asks you about the task, you reply "I'm in over my head" – That is a metaphor for drowning. No wonder you are avoiding the situation. What if you said instead, "I'm building toward something big"?

Coaching is all about increasing awareness so that we have more choice. The key is to make sure your metaphors are moving you forward instead of holding you back.

The language we use when talking to ourselves internally or out loud, forms a huge part of the results we get in life. We often treat our self-talk as something that just happens, however, just like the words we speak out loud, self-talk is 100% our choice.

We Get to Choose What We Focus On

We can't pay attention to everything that's going on around us in any given moment. Our brains are constantly making a choice about where to put our *focus*, whether we realise it or not.

What we focus on determines what we see, what we miss and what we get more of. No one can choose that focus for us. Smoking cigarettes is a classic example. People who smoke focus on the pleasures they associate with smoking in order to continue to inhale cancer causing poison into their lungs. The government uses attention grabbing graphic images about the dangers of smoking—on cigarette packaging and billboard advertising—in an effort to deter smokers from continuing the habit. Despite their best intentions, they actually have no way of making a smoker focus on those images. Each individual gets to choose what they see and what they don't; what they filter in and what they ignore. Most smokers simply choose not to focus on the images.

In a great state, we are focused on what we love: the abundant opportunities and the things we are grateful for. In a poor state all we can see is what is going wrong: our mistakes and what we don't have. Take a moment to notice what you are focused on right now and how that is affecting your state. When you change what you focus on, your state is automatically altered as well.

We Get to Choose Our Physiology

The quickest way to get into a depressed state is to lead with your body. If you don't believe me, just try this: drop your head into your hands, rub your face, and let out a couple of deep sighs. How do you feel? Now by contrast, try marching around the room for thirty seconds with your head up and shoulders back wearing a dopey grin on your face. (No really…you've got to try it!) Notice the difference? What you do with your body totally affects your state. This goes for the clothes you wear, your haircut, cologne, perfume, diet, exercise, sleep, posture, exposure to sunlight, facial expressions, shoulder height, stretching and breathing patterns. As soon as you change any of these, your state automatically changes too. It's all your choice!

We are Not Victims

When we realise just how much choice we have it gives us access to unlimited options. It allows us to be totally resourceful in our own lives rather than to suffer as a victim of the choices everyone else is making. Every time we live with the illusion of having no choice and play victim to our circumstances and the choices of others, we dishonour ourselves. We are totally devaluing and diminishing the wonder of what it means to be a human being.

Questions

- *What is most exciting about the discovery that you really are where you have chosen to be?*

- *What areas of choice have most stuck out to you from this chapter?*

- *What advantages and disadvantages would there be for you to embrace 100% choice?*

Chapter Ten

HOPE

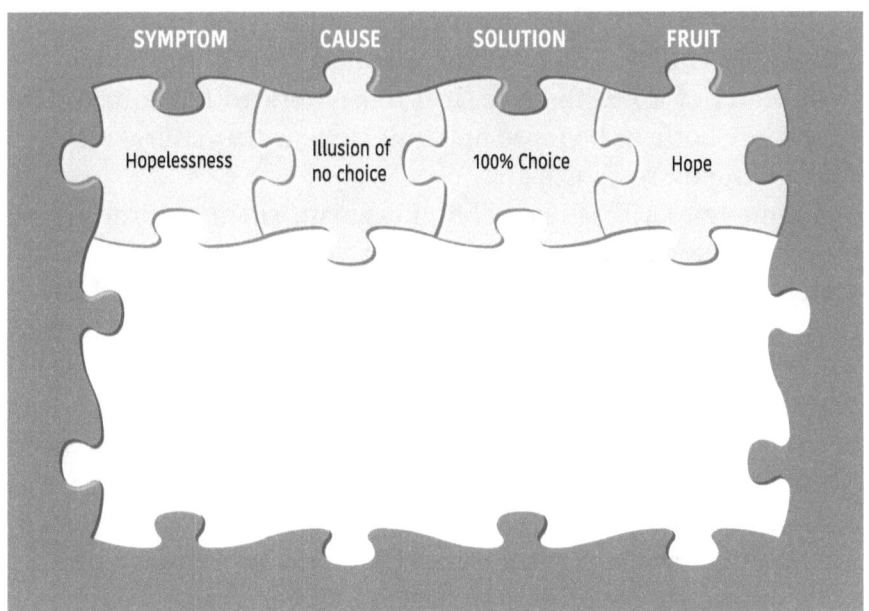

The moment you embrace 100% choice and accept that you are exactly where you have chosen to be, hope comes flooding back. All of a sudden your small, hemmed-in life totally opens up as you become aware of a world of new possibilities, options and opportunities.

Fruit 1: Hope

When you realise that you're exactly where you have chosen to be, it is common to feel one of two things: On the one hand, you may feel confronted, offended and downright horrible when you are unable to escape the fact that you chose this. Yet at the same time, owning this fact can be an incredibly empowering, liberating and joyful moment in your life. The very fact that you chose to be here, means that you have the ability to make other choices to be somewhere else… and hope returns. Whilst ever you believe you are a victim of other people's choices you have no way out. The moment you own your choice to be where you are, you open up a whole realm of possibilities for your future. Hope is the fruit of embracing choice. You can't force fruit to grow, it grows as the by-product of a healthy tree. It doesn't work to tell someone to have more hope or be more hopeful. Hope is the natural result of discovering more choice.

I remember a 'disempowered housewife' client of mine crying tears of joy for over an hour after our very first session. She was gratefully overwhelmed by the knowledge that she had 100% choice. She experienced real hope for change for the first time in 20 years. She had been unhappy for most of that time, yet didn't realise she could do anything about it. Her whole experience had been about suffering the effects of other people's poor choices. Although it was incredibly confronting to realise that she was suffering as a result of her own choices, not due to the choices of her husband, she was at the very same time overwhelmed by the possibilities that lay in front of her now that she had 100% choice.

Hope is linked to choice. Living with the illusion of no choice removes hope. Embracing 100% choice entirely opens up your options. When you have options you find hope. You are no longer stuck. As you embrace 100% choice you will discover that as bad as things may seem, there are still more options. You haven't yet tried everything. There is still a chance to turn this whole thing around. Viktor Frankl survived while millions of his people did not because he never lost hope. Frankyl survived because he never let go of choice. He recognised that he could always choose his state—his reaction to his treatment, his inner meaning—and that made all the difference.

By taking hold of 100% choice, a sense of possibility emerges about what the future holds, no matter how difficult or painful your past may have been. This moves you from what appears to be a very small space to a very large, abundant, wide open space.

Real hope v's false hope

False hope is wishing things would be better but believing deep in your heart that they won't ever improve. It is simply wishing against what you know to be true. It's feeling that you deserve more but knowing you are stuck with your lot in life.

Real hope on the other hand is simply a product of embracing 100% choice.

The moment you live with the illusion of no choice and succumb to the victim mindset, hope evaporates because you are out of options to improve your situation. You have no control and the belief that you have no real choice in the matter.

Wanting, wishing, hoping, longing all while managing a residual disappointment is the experience of false hope. If you remain in this space for too long, it gets inside you and inevitably dials down your expectation of life.

The point of my story is this. Don't confuse yourself by thinking false hope and real hope are the same.

The only way to live with genuine hope is to position yourself with 100% choice and to break out of the illusion of no choice. Sure you don't always get to choose what happens to you, but you do get to choose your response.

The moment you embrace choice, it is impossible to feel stuck! No matter what life throws at you, you always have options about how you will respond.

Questions

- *Have you ever experienced moving from a sense of being stuck and feeling hopeless to having hope about your future again?*

- *What areas of your life could use some fresh hope at the moment?*

- *Can you see how embracing 100% choice in these areas would change the game?*

Chapter Eleven

HELPLESSNESS

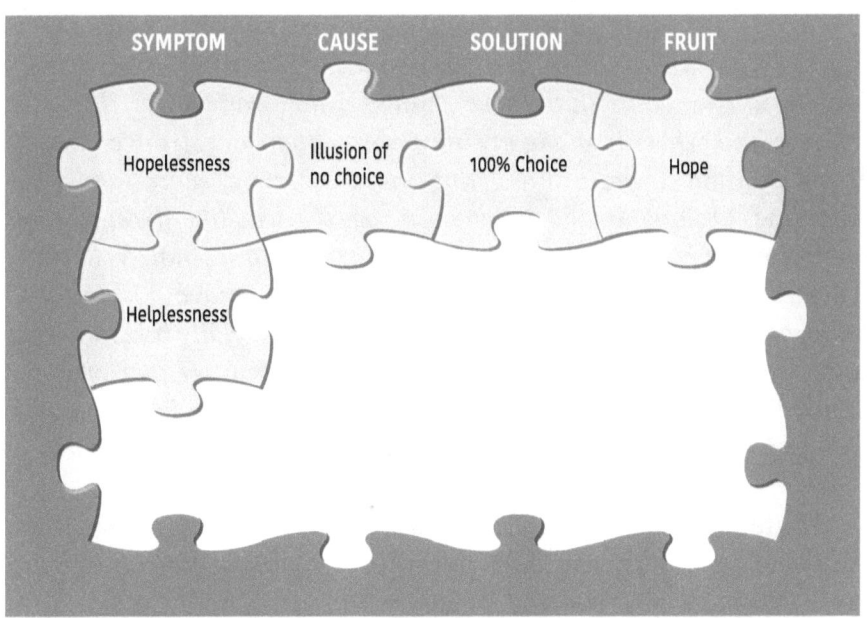

COMMON SYMPTOM NUMBER TWO IS HELPLESSNESS. Exercising 100% choice can be really hard, especially when you feel weak, small or powerless.

Symptom 2: Helplessness

The word helplessness sums up the experience of trying to use choice effectively in your life and finding yourself in direct competition with someone else's (or everyone else's) choices. Helplessness describes what it is like to lack the confidence, ability and belief to actually take control of your results and bring change to your world.

When someone has spent considerable time with the illusion of no choice, they can find it quite challenging to make this new sense of choice work in the real world. If you could get inside their head, you would likely hear them saying: *"Sure, I may have choice, but it's hard to use my choice. Everyone else's choice seems more important than mine. I feel small and insignificant; I need others to change so that I can change. I am waiting for things to change and others to make my life easier. Others are stronger, better, more dominant, more important, more assertive, more intelligent than me. Others have it better than me. If I was like them, then it would be easy to use my choice, but I'm not, so it's not. When my choices come up against others choices, I lose. I have no ability to enforce my choice and hold the space... so I don't really have a choice after all. Well I do have a choice, but I don't want to experience the consequences of making that choice... So I don't really have a choice. It's a nice theory, but it doesn't pan out too well in the real world."*

If life is like a box of chocolates, as Forrest Gump says, then this feeling or experience is like the box getting passed around and everyone else picking what they want first. By the time it gets to you, there is only the orange crème (or Turkish Delight, or whatever one you hate) left. So sure, you get a choice... but it's either the left overs or nothing at all. The struggle to actually use your new found choice in the real world, where there are plenty of others who are far more practiced at exercising choice, can lead to a real sense of helplessness.

Here are some common examples of how this plays out when people begin to embrace their own choice for the first time:

- They are clear about what choice they would like to make, but they feel powerless to live out their choice.
- They want a great marriage, but their husband doesn't share their emotions, so even if they want to have deep conversations, they just get shut down.
- They would love to go to University and study for a career, or a job they've always dreamed of, but their friends and family just don't think it's a good idea.
- They want to have dinner with their kids, and really don't like finishing work after 6pm, but every time they try to tell their boss, he changes the subject.
- They would like to have some time to themselves, but their partner can't look after the kids on the weekend because he plays golf.
- They want to start a family, but their partner strongly believes they just can't afford to right now.
- They want to eat healthily, but their family doesn't want to change their diet. They can't cook two meals each night, one for them and another for the family.
- They want to get to the gym more and take control of their weight, but mum (who also struggles with her weight) feels threatened by this so she actively works against them getting there.
- They want to be happy and have a great social life, but their partner works away at the mines all week and is too tired to go out when they come home for the weekend.
- They want to set aside time to finish their course so they can get a promotion, but they are so busy running the kids to sport and music lessons they often miss out on studying.

Life seems to be all about determinism, fate and chance. You win some and lose some, but ultimately the wind blows where it will and you are powerless to overcome the forces of the universe. It would be easy for you to get stuck at this point in the change journey and go back to feeling hopeless. However, by staying in the judgment free space, remembering that people work perfectly and maintaining an outcomes focus (from part one) you will find that you actually still have great leverage for change. But first, let's take a look at what actually causes this sense of helplessness.

Questions

- *What challenges are you facing at the moment where there are dominant people who seem to have all the power to affect your life?*

- *Which relationships in your world have a power imbalance?*

- *What areas of your life remain stuck, even when you embrace 100% choice?*

Chapter Twelve

GIVING YOUR POWER AWAY

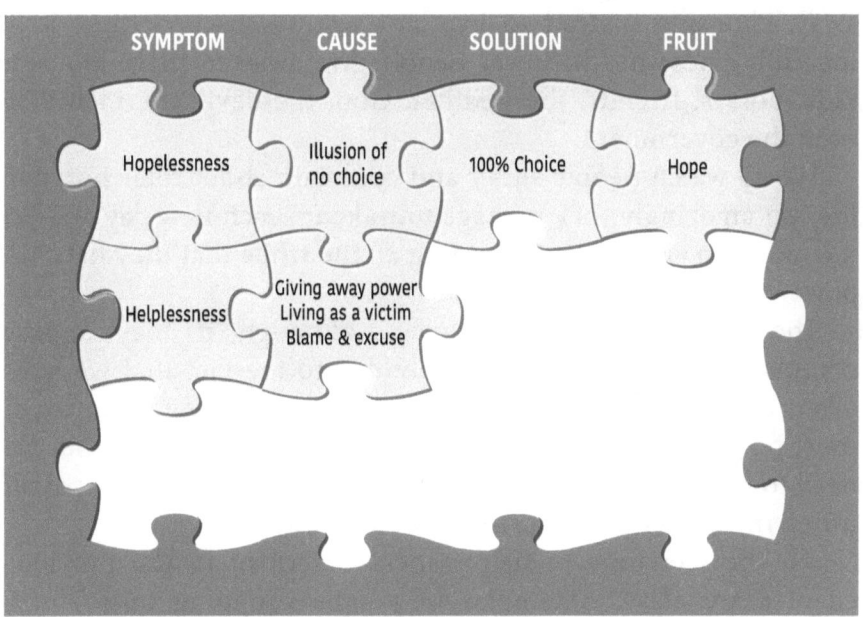

IT TURNS OUT THAT POWER CANNOT BE TAKEN FROM A PERSON. It can only be given away. The root cause of helplessness is living with blame and excuse as a victim.

Cause 2: Giving Away Your Personal Power

There are three things that blow my hair back most in life. Firstly, I am awestruck by how incredibly powerful we are. I mean really… It is staggering what people are capable of when they put their minds to it. We are such creative, intelligent, resourceful beings with the ability to do such extraordinary things. I'm typing away on my laptop computer using my iPhone as an internet hotspot while listening to some sweet tunes through my treasured earphones wondering how in the world we ever worked out how to make this stuff. It's mind blowing!

Even more staggering however, is how much power we give away, choosing instead to live as disempowered victims. It is incredible how much power people give away to their spouses, kids, bosses, friends, the weather, God, the devil, the media or even the government.

We all watch people suffer and complain about their horrible life, yet amazingly they manage to wake up each new day and do it over again and again, imagining all the while that they have no power to change their situation.

The cause of feeling helpless, although it may appear complicated and unique, is simply due to the fact that we have given our power away. No one can take our power from us, it must be given willingly. I know that might sound stupid, but we need to remember that we are not stupid. There has to be a payoff for giving away our power or we wouldn't do it.

All the scenarios of helplessness described in the previous chapter are classic examples of people dropping into 'story'. Story is anything, real or imagined, that becomes an excuse for why we can't get what we want. Underneath our conscious self we have a 'mini me' (our ego, which is represented in much of our self-talk). Mini me is always looking for a story that shows how we were 100% committed to trying, but something outside our control prevented us from actually doing it, so it's not our fault. This strategy is a very clever way of keeping us safe from failure and disappointment. You can't fail if you don't try. There is a pay-off for living as though your choices aren't as important as other people's (people work perfectly remember). You get pity, safety, the moral high ground and a chance to hold resentment and anger. You're allowed to feel self-righteous and deep down you can feel better than those who walk over you.

Blame and Excuse

One of the key ways we give away our power comes though living out of blame and excuse. That is, we imagine that the results we are getting in life are entirely someone else's fault. For example you might say:

- I was born like this—it's my genetics
- I was raised like this—it's parental conditioning
- I am limited by what is happening all around me—it's my environment

Two of the best ways to disempower yourself are *externalization* and *obfuscation*—they are also two fantastic words to have in your vocabulary!

Externalisation is placing all your hope for change on things that are outside of your control, so that you become a passive bystander, or the recipient of whatever comes along in the game of life.

Obfuscation means to cloud the issue, to make it more complicated and unclear than it really is, so that you don't have to actually deal with what is going on. It's like listening to a politician answer a relatively simple question... Ten minutes later they have weaved a trail of mystery, talking about all kinds of rubbish without ever actually answering the question. Complicating issues disempowers us and dilutes our energy, taking our focus away from dealing with our reality.

The Victim

As we saw in Chapter Six—State is King, many people take the Have, Do, Be approach to life. That approach is all about giving away your power and living as a victim. When I HAVE enough time, money, support, energy, resources etc., then I will DO what I know I really want to be doing, and then I will BE happy and successful… the problem is, I DON'T HAVE nearly enough time, money, support or energy and I'm waiting until things change for me. People who are successful in life (or at least more successful than me) have more time, money, support and energy than me. This victim mentality leads to complaining about what we don't have, and Waiting for the planets to align. Until that miraculously happens, we are stuck living in an incredibly disempowered and helpless state.

Now that we see how giving our power away is the cause of helplessness, let's move on and explore the solution.

Questions

- *Who or what have you given power to?*

- *What payoff do you get for giving this power away?*

- *Who or what do you blame for your current circumstances or results?*

- *Are there any excuses you use to explain why your life is the way it is?*

Chapter Thirteen

TAKING 100% RESPONSIBILITY

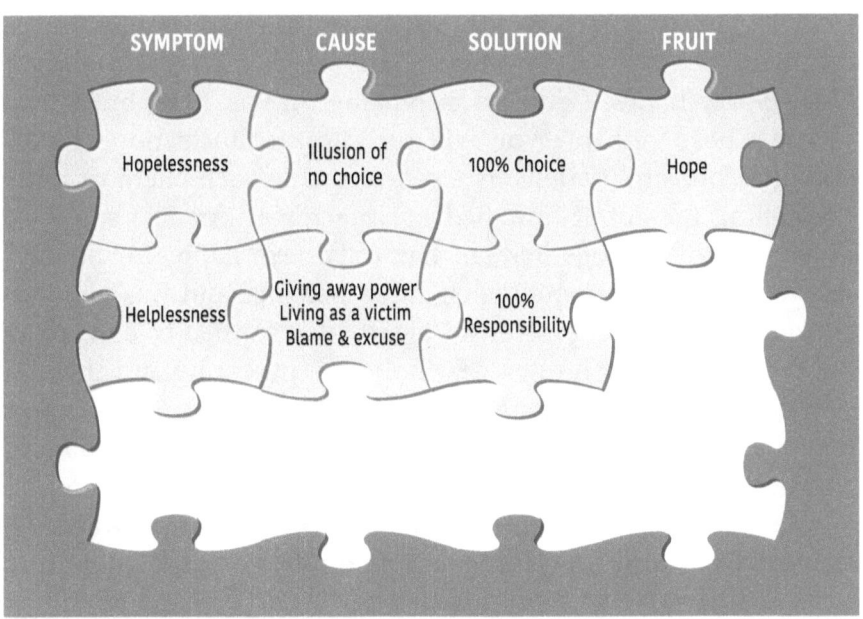

THE WAY OUT OF HELPLESSNESS IS TO TAKE 100% RESPONSIBILITY for your life and your results. Your results are exactly that… yours!

Solution 2: Taking 100% responsibility

When someone complains that they are not a creative person I love to ask them, "Can you tell me who is creating your reality then?" Of course we are creative—it is the image of the divine in us. Every time we open our mouths we are having conversations that have never been had before in the history of the world. All day we create ideas, thoughts, sentences, relationships and experiences, not to mention more intentional creations of art, music and science. We create our reality by the choices we make. We are not victims of our external world, pawns tossed to and fro by the forces of fate and chance. *We are in control of us.*

It is not uncommon for the disempowered housewife to complain about being treated poorly by her husband and or kids. (Sorry ladies, I admit I'm picking on you here, but if you will just bear with me you will see a great illustration of how taking responsibility delivers freedom). One such client of mine was telling me about how bad her marriage was. She said that in 30 years of life together, she had only been happy for the first six weeks. After that she realised that her husband was going to be 'large and in charge'. He was clearly determined to control all the decisions about money, sex, holidays, parenting and the T.V. channel. With tears flowing freely she told me story after story of how horribly unfair it was and then asked, "When is he going to change and love me the way a husband ought to love his wife?"

What a funny question! Change? Why in the world would he change? His world is perfect—and no doubt he boasts about it to all his friends. He gets what he wants, when he wants it, and he has a personal assistant (aka wifey) to make it all happen for him at the snap of his fingers! There is zero motivation on his part to change such an ideal set up. I told this lady that despite whatever she may have believed for the past 30 years, no one was forcing her to be a helpless victim with no hope or power. If she wasn't happy with the way her life was set up and the way she was being treated, she should simply change it. I said, "Stop blaming your husband for treating you so poorly and start taking responsibility for the fact that you have trained him to treat you like this for the last 30 years!"

I vividly recall a similar scenario from a ten minute snippet of a Dr. Phil episode that I caught while flicking channels one lunchtime. The good doctor was counselling a couple that had been having some significant marital issues. The husband had a history of having affairs, and had just been caught out in his fifth extramarital relationship. His wife was devastated and didn't know if she could find a way to forgive him and go on. He was so sorry and couldn't explain how he had slipped up like this again. Dr. Phil turned to the wife and said in his southern-American accent, "Honey… do you know why your husband has had these five affairs?" (You'll need to re-read that line with the southern accent.) The wife replied that she had no idea, but said she was desperate to finally understand. Phil continued, "Because he can… you make it OK. If you don't want him to have any more affairs, don't let him."

We are constantly training others how to treat us by what we allow and deny. What seemed so complicated and unique to the wife a minute ago was now very simple. He moved her out of helplessness by giving her 100% responsibility for the outcome she was getting. No blame. No judgment. Just responsibility. We are each 100% responsible for the results we are getting and for the results we would like to be getting.

Proactivity

One of the key differences we see in people who take responsibility for their outcomes is that they are *proactive* rather than *reactive*. The word 'proactive' means taking action before hand or ahead of time, whereas to be 'reactive' means to act after the event or in response to what has happened.

The proactive person decides that today will be a fruitful and effective day filled with incredible opportunities, while the reactive person will wait and see how effective the day is, and decide after it has happened to them. The reactive person lives at the effect of the climate and temperature of the world around them. The proactive person takes their own weather with them.

Letting Go of Our Old Friends 'Blame' and 'Excuse'

The advantage of living with blame and excuse is that it is never our fault and never our responsibility. It is much easier to live with blame and excuse than to take hold of 100% responsibility and choice because when you do that the buck stops with you!

You are well within your right to go on living out of blame and excuse, choosing to blame others for treating you poorly. It's a very natural thing to do. However, even if this approach makes sense and can be perfectly justified, it has no ability to get you any outcome other than the one you are currently experiencing. Results only change when we take responsibility for the way they are and the way we'd like them to be.

Questions

- *What are the advantages and disadvantages for letting go of blame and excuse and taking hold of 100% responsibility and choice?*

- *Seeing that taking responsibility is by far the more difficult path, what would really motivate a person to keep choosing this approach rather than taking the 'easy way out'?*

Chapter Fourteen

PERSONAL POWER

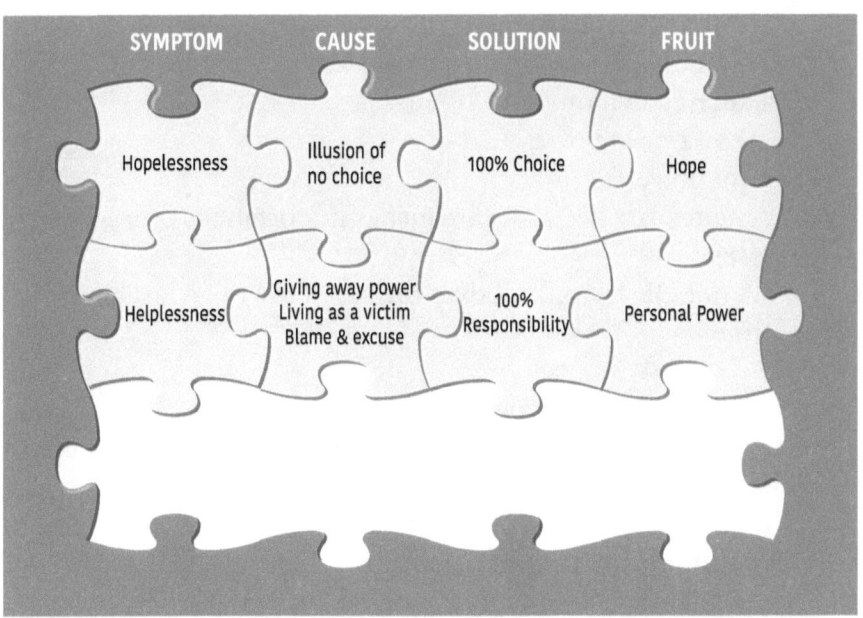

W**HEN YOU EMBRACE 100% RESPONSIBILITY FOR YOUR LIFE, you get your power back.**

Fruit 2: Personal Power

The discovery that you have 100% choice and total responsibility for your own results and relationships, can be an extraordinarily empowering. The fruit of this is a sense of personal power. Not only do you see that you have the ability to make choice, but you also have the power to do so. You realise that you actually have the ability to control your world. You discover, maybe for the first time, that you can make change.

When this happens you may start to hear yourself saying things like:

- I am not helpless
- I am not a victim
- Wow! I have power
- I am powerful
- I matter, my decisions are just as important as everyone else's
- It's not OK to walk all over me or for me to go last all the time

Do you realise how powerful you are? You are the only one capable of blocking your success and the only one who is able to set yourself free. Just beyond what you can't do is what you can do!

It is common for people to position themselves as victims of their world feeling as though they have no real power to change the way things are. The game totally changes when people realise that while blame and excuse are kind of fun, they don't really make sense. Remember life is not based on what happens to us, but on the meaning we place on these things. You are not just an actor in a story someone else has written, but you really are the storyteller.

When people really come to terms with this, they start to get a sense of just how powerful they really are. No one really has the power to destroy your life or ruin your dreams unless you let them. And no one really has the power to make you happy and successful. Its all you!

Taking your power back

In order to take your power back, you have to be willing to let go of the payoff you got for giving it away in the first place. As we've already seen, people that feel incredibly disempowered often believe they have had their power taken away from them by others. Yet interestingly personal power can never be stolen, it is only ever given away. The only reason we would give it away is if we get something valuable in return.

Embracing 100% choice and responsibility for your own life is hard! It is far safer and easier to blame someone or something else for your results. The main pay off for giving away your power is that nothing is your responsibility or your fault. You can hide away from the world and never put yourself out there, which means you can't fail, get rejected, or be disappointed. Playing the victim also gives you pity and allows you to take the moral high ground in order to feel good about yourself.

Remember, there are always rewards for living in dysfunction. That's why people do it. If you are willing to swap these rewards (secondary gains) for something more resourceful, you can take your power back today.

Creating a life you don't need an escape from

In order to fully flourish, the aim of the game is to create a life you don't need an escape from. All addiction, and the majority of sickness is all about escape. At a cellular level we are all hardwired to avoid pain and pursue pleasure. The reason why substances and certain practices become addictive is because of the power they have to give us instant pain avoidance or instant pleasure.

All addiction is birthed out of the desire to escape the pain of our current situation and to deal with the discomfort of the real world. Everything we do is in some way an attempt to bring peace and comfort to ourselves.

The vast majority of sickness is also simply about escape. If we find ourselves stuck in situations that are dysfunctional or painful and we are not making a believable plan to change them, then for the sake of love, our subconscious will find an exit strategy for us. In our busy world, it is not ok to rest unless you are sick. Being ill can provide a break from the heavy responsibility of living in a life you are not enjoying and feel powerless to change.

Therefore, the more we take full responsibility for directing and shaping our own lives, the less we need to escape from the feeling of being a victim to a life created by someone else. Embracing 100% choice also means you are 100% responsible for choosing your experience in every moment. If you don't like your current experience, change it rather than seek to escape from it. Drugs, food, pornography and work are the addictions of our day. Rather than fighting the addiction, address the reason the addiction is needed. The key is to create a life you don't need an escape from.

What do you want again?

Focusing on your desired outcomes becomes very important again at this point. A new found sense of personal power often comes with a much bigger sense of the potential to have the ideal life rather than just settle for what previously seemed to be your lot in life.

It's a great chance to revisit these key questions:

- What do you want?
- What would you like to have happen?
- What would excite you?

- What is the dream?
- If everything was as it should be for you?"
- What would you be doing/seeing/having etc?

With a sense of *power* comes the chance to bring about change. It now becomes possible to create a new "program" for your life, find a new story to live out of and experience new and improved results. A new wave of possibility starts to wash over you. This is a very exciting yet quite dangerous stage. Walking in this newly empowered state can leave you vulnerable to hurt and pain if you have not properly prepared for the responses you will get from others as you start to take your power back.

In the next chapter we will begin exploring the final layer of the model which will prepare you for this next stage of the journey.

Questions

- *If you had a strong sense of personal power, what would you do that you are currently waiting for others to do for you?*

- *Do you see any dangers associated with feeling powerful rather than being a victim?*

- *What would it look like for you to create a life you don't need an escape from?*

Chapter Fifteen

HURTFULNESS

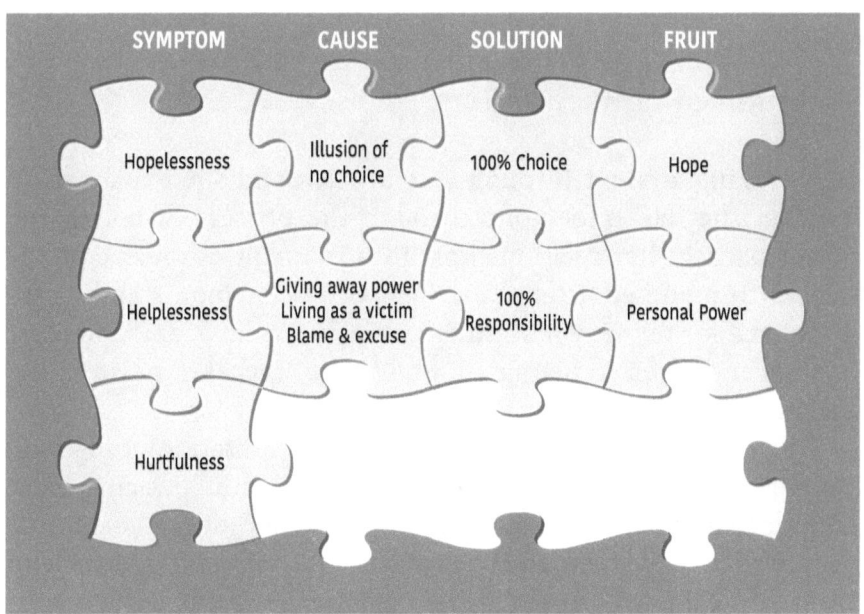

WHEN YOU USE YOUR POWER IN THE REAL WORLD, IT OFTEN places you in direct conflict with those who have held power over you in the past. Unless you are well prepared for the battle, you lose and end up getting hurt.

Symptom 3: Hurtfulness

Hurtfulness sums up the pain we experience when trying to take back the power from those people in life who exert power over us in some way. It's one thing to realise you have choice and responsibility, it's another thing entirely to hang on to it when others try and take it from you. Those who have held power over you don't enjoy the process of being retrained and they tend to fight to hang onto it. Taking your power back always comes at a price. The question is; are you prepared for the fight, or will hurtfulness cause you to go back up the symptom chain through helplessness and hopelessness again?

The pain of confrontation

I was taking a client through this process and she explained to me that she had once gone through the process of taking the power back in her relationships. In a moment of great courage she confronted her sister about her poor behaviour, standing up for herself for the very first time. Twenty years later, and her sister had never spoken to her again! She said to me, "I'm never doing that again... look where that got me!"

Due to the pain and hurtfulness of confrontation going bad, people often resort to settling for far less and lowering their relational standards. It just seems too hard and unrealistic to see people change. The only real alternative to confronting those who are treating you poorly is to allow these powerful people in your world to behave how ever they please. No matter how hurtful it is, you just have to cope with it.

When you settle with hurtfulness for long enough, it becomes the new normal. In order to survive requires you to distort how happy you really are and suppress the pain deeper and deeper.

I saw some high quality Facebook wisdom down this line recently. "The best way not to get hurt by others is to have no expectations."

It definitely is one way not to get hurt, but I promise you there are far better ways…

Before using your power in the world, it is important to carefully consider all the costs involved. Are you willing to part with all the benefits and rewards of being a disempowered victim? There are many people who have gone before you who've made it this far and then turned back because it all got too hard.

When you start taking responsibility for your life and making changes to how you'd like things to be, there is always push back from your world that feel very personal and painful! Your initial attempts at assertiveness can leave you coming off second best as those who are used to having the power don't like giving it back. If you've ever tried to retrain someone to treat to you better, it can be very frustrating, emotionally taxing and personally hurtful.

Let's look at how this plays out with the disempowered housewife. She arrives home after a very empowering and life giving coaching session, ready to lead some significant change in the home. She waits for an opportune moment and begins a serious, but gentle, conversation with her husband about the fact that she is really not happy with how their relationship is going. It's a great start, but things go downhill fast. Trying to maintain her composure, she holds her ground and lets him know that she really is serious about things needing to be different. The conversation starts to escalate. He's got a lot to protect here and is so much better at this game than she is. He knows the exact buttons to press to undermine her progress and get her to back down. He has zero motivation for change right now, so he naturally resists it. He questions her motives and plays some counterattack moves of his own. She knows she is losing the power and feels a wave of hurt and frustration before retreating in a pool of tears.

This type of scenario can play out in any interpersonal relationship where there has been an imbalance of power and the disempowered person embarks on the retraining process. For example, parents retraining kids, kids retraining parents, setting boundaries with friends, employees or employers.

Woundedness

Another way of describing this concept of hurtfulness is to call it *woundedness*. So much of the mess and madness that happens in the world today comes out of our deep sense of woundedness. It is natural in the process of our development to seek to define ourselves as separate from those around us. I am not my family or friends, town, city and country. But who am I? What does it mean to be me? As we start to define our boundaries we are placed in direct conflict with our world and others seeking to do the same thing in their own lives. When we stand up for ourselves we often get hurt. Our hearts get wounded. We find the world to be dangerous, violent and unfair. It pushes back against our attempts at self-definition. Our naivety creates a vulnerability, and that vulnerability gets taken advantage of, causing us to end up hurt, damaged, wounded, broken, calloused, bitter and resentful.

The result is that we live our lives, walk out our relationships, work our careers and conduct our hobbies from this place of woundedness. We live with a deep sense of mistrust of others, behaving guarded and suspicious. We deeply desire happiness but honestly feel that it is a myth.

Woundedness pushes us back into helplessness and ultimately hopelessness. It embeds the fear that change is beyond our reach. Instead of chasing what we want, we settle with what we can get and make the best of our sorry lot in life.

Accused of being wrong

Another classic example of hurtfulness happens when people are accused of doing something wrong and they find great difficulty apologising. I'm sure we all know someone who has no reverse gear and never backs down even when they are wrong. (Or perhaps this may even describe you?)

One of the main reasons people find it so hard to apologise for making mistakes is that everything becomes so personal very quickly. They believe being proven to be wrong says something about them as a person. It's like - if I've been shown to have done something wrong or bad, then I must be wrong or bad. Saying sorry then, would be admitting that they are no good. Therefore, the cost of being wrong becomes way too high and it becomes impossible to apologise.

Instead the accusation becomes very hurtful to their ego and reputation and so they must defend themselves and cover any vulnerability so they don't get hurt any further!

Sometimes this defence even takes the form of attack! Often people who struggle to apologise are great at shifting the focus and the blaming others as quickly as possible.

We'll explore the root cause of this issue and all the other forms of hurtfulness in the next chapter.

Questions

- *Has being assertive ever resulted in you coming off second best?*

- *What areas of your life/work/relationships do you find yourself taking things to heart?*

- *Are there people in your world who leave you feeling frustrated, misunderstood or devalued even when you try to stand up to them?*

- *Where are the greatest areas of obligation in your life?*

- *How well do you apologise when you've made a mistake or are clearly wrong?*

Chapter Sixteen

NEEDINESS

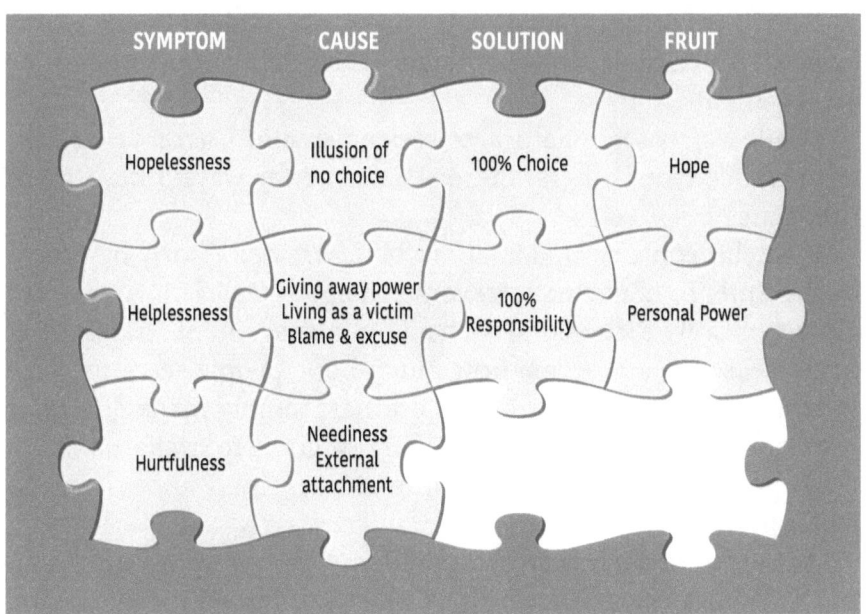

The root cause of hurtfulness is neediness. When you need something from someone else, they have the power to withhold it from you and therefore cause you pain.

Cause 3: Neediness

Putting someone else in charge of meeting your deepest needs for love, significance and self worth is a dangerous thing to do. The moment you need something from someone else, you hand them the power to control your emotional state. They have the power to make you feel great and also to make you feel terrible. Their ability to exert power over you comes from their capacity to withhold from you the thing that you need. When you outsource the meeting of these needs to your world, you place yourself at the mercy of others. When you don't get what you need, you are instantly in a position of lack and pain.

Neediness comes from having your sense of identity and worth externally attached to your roles, relationship, possessions or achievements.

While it may seem natural to seek affirmation, acceptance, and significance from others, there is a far better way to have these needs met.

I watch people complain about being treated poorly by others all the time. To make matters worse, their strategies for change are almost entirely focussed on behaviour management strategies! It never ceases to amaze me how much hope people seem to place in strategies for change that rely on them simply managing their behaviour. They tell themselves, "I'm just going to try harder... I'm really going to focus on responding differently... I know I can do better at this."

As you've read already, the problem with this approach is that the behaviour is simply a fruit of what is going on inside. Trying to manage behaviour is like putting sides back on boxes (as we discussed in Chapter Four—People Work Perfectly).

The pain of neediness

When you live from a position of neediness, it is inevitable that you will also be experiencing some or all of the following situations:

- Working in a job you don't like
- Getting treated poorly by others
- Settling for less money than you are worth
- Working longer hours than they'd like due to other people's incompetence
- Staying in dysfunctional or even abusive relationships
- Being taken advantage of or walked all over
- Doing things out of obligation
- Being unable to say no

There is always a payoff

People remain in situations that they don't like because they get something from them. There must be a reward or else they would have already changed.

When you're in the midst of such a situation it seems so complicated and unique, yet the painfully simple issue underlying each one of these situations is neediness. You stay in a hurtful situation because at the same time it is meeting your needs. Offensive but true…#Sorrynotsorry.

Neediness is typically motivated by a desire for validation, significance, approval and self-worth. Deriving your sense of happiness and worth from other people's approval works really well until the moment they disapprove. Then your world comes crashing down and you find yourself scrambling to back down, giving in or conforming to their expectations to keep them happy so as to regain their approval.

You cannot afford to do anything different because then your needs would not get met! There is no plan B.

We all want to feel good about ourselves and feel that we are valuable and worthwhile. Most of the time our only strategy for meeting this need is through our external world. We find ourselves getting validation and significance from our roles, relationships and possessions. Our massive dependence on these things to provide happiness and self-worth leaves us feeling needy and vulnerable, because our value as a person becomes tied to something outside ourselves, something that we ultimately cannot control.

Getting to sleep at night

I was coaching a middle-aged man about his marriage issues using this framework for change. He kept complaining about how badly his wife was treating him saying, "It just cannot go on like this. Something has to change!"

"Unfortunately, that's just not true" I replied. Of course he could keep going on this way. If it was really so bad being treated like this by his wife, he would have walked away a long time ago. I told him that it was plainly obvious he needed his wife to treat him poorly in order for him sleep at night!

I don't care…It's not my marriage. But let's have the honest conversation.

People work perfectly remember, there must be some payoff for continuing to tolerate being treated in a way that he says is so offensive. Eckhart Tolle says "To complain makes no sense. Accept the situation, change it or leave it. All else is madness"

Here is how this works. In order to get to sleep each night, we must consciously or subconsciously be able to square away with ourselves that we are a decent person. To feel as though you are a bad person or of no value is a very dark and horrific place full of shame, guilt and anxiety. If your head hits the pillow at night feeling like this, how could you possibly sleep! It reminds me of the old phrase - There is no rest for the wicked! We will do absolutely everything possible to avoid coming face to face with this reality.

Because we are so desperate to know that we are 'a good person', we will go to great lengths to prove this to ourselves and others. Unfortunately, these strategies are frequently external, really unresourceful and come at a high price.

Here are some classic examples of the different approaches people take based on their character type:

1. *The people pleaser*—If the people in their world are happy with them, they feel good about themselves, but if others are displeased with them or something they've done, they feel terrible. In order to make sure everyone in their world is happy with them requires them to say yes to everyone's demands and never confront the things they do that upset or offend them. The people pleaser is constantly putting a smile on their face despite the fact they are wearing huge personal costs.

2. *The peace keeper*—They get to give themselves a tick in the 'I'm a good person' box when they find creative ways to resolve other people's problems by accommodating to their demands. This strategy involves smoothing things over and sweeping things under the mat to keep up the illusion that everything is OK. Conflict is to be avoided at all costs and so issues never actually get resolved.

3. *The martyr/saint*—They need to keep themselves surrounded by people that behave worse than they do. This gives a clear reference point to prove by comparison, that they are better than other people. This also gives them the moral high ground and makes them feel like a good person. The martyr also gets extra brownie points for what horrible behaviour they can tolerate and yet still function in life with a smile on

their face. People in this situation need to be treated badly (and tell others about it) so that they can feel good about themselves and get to sleep at night. If they were surrounded by happy, healthy people, they would not have anyone worse to compare themselves to and would end up feeling inadequate and insecure.

4. *The hero*—They need to find people to rescue. They are constantly surrounded by victims and needy people who suck them dry, yet the validation and kudos they get by solving others needs fills their cup and proves they are a good person.

5. *The bully*—They constantly find evidence of others flaws and weakness while hiding behind their areas of personal strength. Road rage, teasing, violence and abuse are all examples of the ego trying to bolster itself by putting others down. It is another unresourceful comparison strategy of needing to be better than others in order to feel good about yourself. The bully constantly judges everyone and everything and is full of self righteousness.

Comparing Yourself with Others

Comparing ourselves with others is all about external neediness. It is the root cause of so much of the pain and hurt we suffer in life. Eckhart Tolle says that one of the key strategies of our ego is to prop ourselves up using comparison. We need to find examples of people who are behaving worse than us to feel like we are decent people.[36]

I coached a guy who had been a chronic road-rager for almost 30 years. His behaviour was so bad that his wife had refused to travel with him. In his mind the issue was simply about anger management and the way forward was to learn patience, and practice forgiveness and being kind to others. Surprisingly though, his behaviour management strategies had been entirely unsuccessful. Every time his self control eventually wore thin and he resorted back to being a wild man whose blood boils at the first sign of poor driving!

Our coaching conversations revolved around the fact that the road rage was just the fruit of his external strategy for feeling good about himself. We explored the idea that, due to a deep insecurity about his own inherent value and worth, his ego needed to be bolstered by finding examples of people who were worse than him. This comparison enabled him to subconsciously feel superior to them, meaning he must be OK. In defending his position he said, "Yeah, but there are so many 'dickheads' on the road. Every time I get in the car there are bad drivers all around me threatening to take me out! It's just shocking how bad drivers are these days."

I honestly replied that I couldn't remember the last time I'd seen an example of poor driving, and that I always had pleasant experiences of being on the road with courteous, safe drivers around me. It was as if he needed to find 'dickheads' to make himself feel superior, so his subconscious made sure that was exactly what he discovered. Even when people drove safely, he found a way of distorting what he saw to gain more evidence for what he needed to believe.

As soon as he dealt with the core issue, by replacing his external strategy with a new internal one, there was no longer anything he needed to prove or defend. He wasn't so needy and the road rage fell away.

Needing Your Parent's Approval

One of the most significant and damaging arenas neediness plays out in is the relationship we have with our parents. So much hurtfulness is caused by people desperately needing (and not getting) their parents approval.

One of my clients had only ever defined success in terms of an annual salary and net worth. His father had set this clear figure for him some 30 years prior and even though he had worked incredibly hard his whole life, this guy had still never quite reached the mark.

The craziest thing about the story was that his dad had been dead for almost ten years and yet he was still driving himself to prove his success as measured by his dad's standard. His sincere belief was that his dad had gone to his grave feeling like his son was a major failure and nothing but a disappointment. Driven by this belief, he was determined to prove his father wrong. He was so desperate and needy for his father's approval that he continued to fight for it, even though it was impossible to get it.

I have friends well into their forties, whose parents opinion is still the most important voice in their life! In fact it is common for people to still be trying to keep their parents happy and get their approval their whole life.

Negotiability

We all like to think we are highly negotiable; however, when we are needy, we give away our negotiating power. I'll never forget the first time I discovered that people often imagine they are far more negotiable than they really are. A 50 year old man asked me to coach him through a key life decision he was facing. On the surface, it appeared that he had two clear options on the table. He wanted help to see which path would suit him best. It quickly became evident, however, that he was totally attached to Option B and needed to make it work, even though we could both see it was not the right decision for him. It was so fascinating watching him distort his own feeling on the subject.

The two options he was considering were: A) stay in the country he loved, in the job he loved and remain single for the time being; or B) move countries and live in a city that terrifies him, to pursue a relationship with a woman who he knows deep down doesn't really love him and will only seek to control and dominate him. Um… Jeez that's a tough one!

The problem was that he felt like he needed Option B to work out so he could prove to himself that he was a good man and worth loving. If he couldn't make that option work it would confirm his worst fears about his own lack of value. Madness…It is the only word that could describe this situation!

Another great example of neediness undermining negotiability is watching a parent negotiate with a two year old in the lolly aisle of the supermarket. This is such an interesting example because the power imbalance is so dramatic. The parent is bigger, older, smarter, wiser and stronger, but against all the odds something amazing happens. Even though the parent owns all the money, the house, the clothes and the food; they drive the car, pay the electricity bill and have absolutely everything the child needs… the two year old has all the power! How amazing.

Let's play out the scenario. The two year old decides that his life will not be complete without a chocolate bar. Mum gently explains that they have just had breakfast and, if he can just wait a little longer, she will make him a honey sandwich and he can sit down to watch playschool as soon as they get home. That option fails to alter the kid's attachment to the chocolate bar and the situation escalates. Wheeling your trolley past, you know full well how this will end. Not only will the little monkey get the chocolate bar, he will also get a banana milk and mum will make him a honey sandwich when they get home!

So why does mum give all the power to her toddler? Is it because it is just easier to say yes? Or maybe she just wants peace? Maybe she is embarrassed about creating a scene and having everyone judge her parenting. These are all good reasons, but I assure you none of them have the power to drive this kind of parenting behaviour. So what is it? What does she get in exchange for the chocolate bar, for giving in? The truth is she needs her child to like her. If he is upset with her, she feels like a bad mother and more importantly, like a bad person. She has to tolerate his tantrum. Even though she tries to hold the power, the moment he threatens to withdraw his love and affection she must back down and give in.

So many apparently complex and unique people issues come back to this same root cause. We tie our identity with our external world. We identify with things, roles, relationships, achievements and possessions. Our ego strains to validate itself through these external attachments.

Neediness = hurtfulness

All neediness ends up leading to hurtfulness:

> I need you to like me
> I need you to accept me
> I need you to validate my decisions
> I need your approval
> I need you to agree with me
> I need you to tell me I'm valuable
> I need you to support me
> I need you to employ me
> I need you to say yes to me
> I need you to give me pity
> I need you to believe in me
> I need you to tell me I'm right

The moment you don't get what you need, you are in a world of hurt.

Underneath every emotional, physical, relational and even financial pain is some kind of limiting belief about our own inadequacy, which causes us to be needy. We are desperate to feel loved and accepted, but terrified that we wont be. So much angst, frustration and dysfunction in life comes out of our own insecurity about trying to prove our worth to the world, or by trying to defend our ego in the face of perceived threats. Basing your opinion of yourself on the approval and acceptance of others is a wonderful plan…until the moment someone disapproves of you and doesn't accept you, and then you instantly suffer. Yet, what if there was nothing to prove and nothing to defend? What if you were able to show up in the world present and unguarded? The key is always to take 100% ownership for your own value and worth as a human being rather than outsourcing that decision to your world based on whether you can meet their expectations. This is the very next piece in the puzzle.

Questions

- *Who or what has the ability to hurt you?*
- *How would you describe your relationship with your parents?*
- *Do you define yourself by what you do, what you have, or who you are?*
- *How attached to your roles and relationships are you?*
- *Do you find yourself compromising and backing down when others withhold their approval or acceptance of you?*
- *Which, (if any) of the five character types best describes you?*

Chapter Seventeen

100% OWNERSHIP

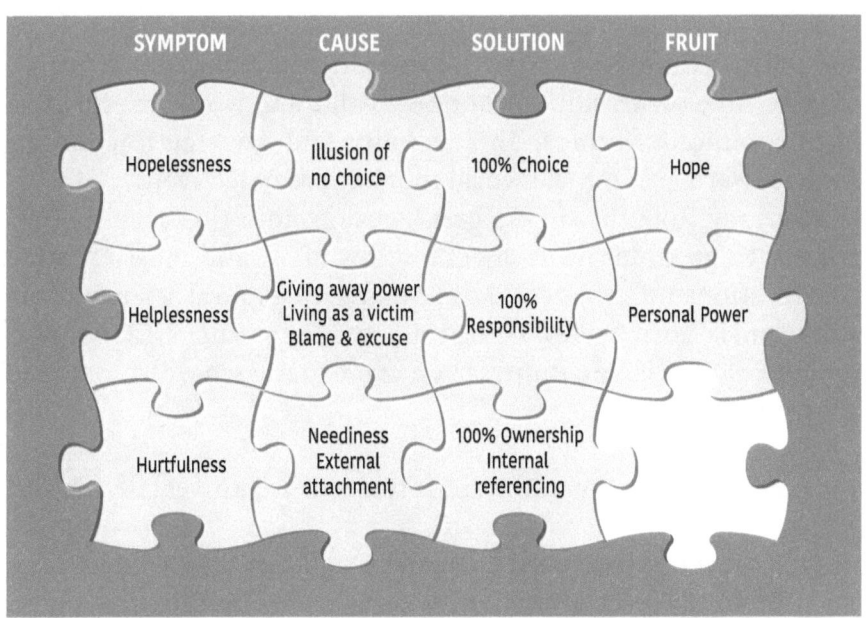

THE WAY OUT OF HURTFULNESS IS TO TAKE 100% OWNERSHIP of your own value and worth. This is done by meeting your needs internally, rather than seeking them to be met externally.

Solution 3: 100% Ownership

The very moment you no longer need stuff from the people who cause you so much grief, the hurtfulness instantly drops away. They have no more leverage to hurt you or cause you to remain in horrible situations that are killing you. You get to go free. There is nothing to prove, and nothing to defend. Everything becomes so much less personal.

When you first step up and try to use your personal power in the real world, you will often end up facing direct confrontation with those who have held power over you, and that can feel like a personal attack. The way forward is to let go of needing the approval and acceptance of others as your source of significance and self-worth and replace that with an internal reference. It is time to take 100% ownership of your own value and worth irrespective of the opinion of others. This will give you amazing freedom to walk forward and see the world much more objectively.

Anthony Robbins speaks great wisdom into this very space.[37] In fact, I'd go so far as to say one of his finest and most valuable contributions into the realm of human behavioural science is his work on six core needs. This idea provides a crucial foundation for addressing the hurtfulness you can experience when you take your power back.

Here is a summary of the six core needs we universally share:

1. *Certainty*—the need for safety, comfort and control. The need for certainty will cause us to do our best to avoid chaos and the unexpected. It will cause us to consider the risks or potential danger of a situation before taking action.
2. *Uncertainty*—the need for variety, adventure, change and the need to experience new things. If we have 100% certainty, we become bored and if we have 100% variety we become very unsettled. Both needs are equally important and will find a way of being met.

3. *Significance*—the need for a sense of independence, value, self-worth and importance. It drives us to assert ourselves as individuals, look out for our own interests and put our own ego at the fore.
4. *Love and connection*—the need for meaningful relationships, connectedness, and interdependence as relational beings. We are motivated to share and develop relationships with people to meet this need in our lives. Yet, if we are always defined by our relationships we can feel smothered and crave personal space to be alone.
5. *Contribution*—this is our need to give back, add value, make a difference and leave a legacy. Even in a very consumer driven society each of us have an innate desire to give back in some way. Contribution is about sharing what we have with others and seeking to add value.
6. *Growth*—this is our need to become, reach our potential and achieve what is possible. This core need is what compels us to mature and evolve as human beings.

Resourceful or Unresourceful

Understanding that these needs will always be met one way or other in your life is vitally important. The issue isn't whether or not they will be met, but how they will be met. The key is to find resourceful, healthy ways of meeting these needs, rather than unresourceful ways. Instead of labelling the behaviour as good or bad, right or wrong, it is better assessed by how useful it is to your overall aims. Here are some examples of how people may go about meeting their six core needs in either resourceful or unresourceful ways.

NEED	UNRESOURCEFUL	RESOURCEFUL
CERTAINTY *comfort, safety, control*	Controlling others, bullying, busyness, perfectionism, fear of the unknown, fear of failure, risk aversion, playing it safe, anxiety, junk food, pornography, self-righteousness, religious pride, arrogance, hoarding, remaining in unhappy situations because of the security they provide, addiction, self-medication, self-sabotage, anxiety.	Backing ourselves, embracing uncertainty, good routines, rituals, setting plans/goals, self-discipline, creativity, helpful habits, mantras, dressing well, eating healthily, exercise, confidence.
VARIETY *newness, uncertainty, change, surprise, adventure*	Substance abuse, being a party animal, recklessness, busyness, self-sabotage, creating drama, constant change, being an adrenaline junky, affairs, crime.	Planned adventure, spontaneity, hobbies, creativity, meeting new people, planned variety, sport, holidays.
SIGNIFICANCE *importance, worth, value, independence, individuality*	Putting others down, judgment, lying, victimhood, rebellion, neediness, busyness, performance, attachments, comparison, notoriety, arrogance, narcissism, and codependence.	Taking responsibility for your own significance, choosing to value yourself, 100% ownership, honour, 'I am significant.'
LOVE/ CONNECTION *meaningful relationships*	Neediness, self-harming, unhealthy relationships, busyness, connection through drama, codependence, drug and alcohol problems, shallow relationships, conforming in order to fit in, promiscuity.	Self-love, real relationships, serving others.
CONTRIBUTION *give back, add value, legacy, influence*	Being a workaholic, busyness, needing to be seen and recognised by others, contributing inappropriately, doing too much.	Service, love, generosity, giving without the need for reward, adding value, giving appropriately.
GROWTH *become, achieve, enlarge, attain, realise potential*	Growth in one area that is out of proportion with all other areas, obsessions, drivenness, growth without direction, obesity, negative emotions.	Progress, momentum, direction, improvement, character formation, knowing what you want, directed growth.

There are four key insights about how these needs operate in our lives that must be understood to make this model really work.

1. These six needs operate in a *vacuum* in our lives. That means they will be filled one way or another. If we do not have an intentional plan to meet our needs resourcefully, we will inevitably think of, or adopt unresourceful behaviour to meet that need.
2. *Don't stop it, swap it.* Because needs operate in a vacuum, we can't just stop it. In order to change any unresourceful behaviour in our life we must choose to replace it with a resourceful behaviour that meets the same need. If we simply stop it, we will end up doing something equally unresourceful, if not worse, to meet the underlying need.
3. *Needs trump values.* Because our needs cannot go unmet, we may find ourselves doing things that violate that which is most important to us. This is often why good people do bad things. Why people who value honesty, lie; people who value integrity, cheat; and people who value health, smoke.
4. *Every negative behaviour has a positive intent.* Remember, people are not their behaviour. We engage in bad behaviour because we are needy people, not because we are bad people. We are capable of making poor choices and hurting ourselves and others. The object is not to try to overcome our needs, but rather to find high-quality ways of meeting our needs; ways that are congruent with our values.

Lasting change happens when we replace unresourceful behavioural strategies with new ones that meet the original intention and also are aligned to our personal values.

Internal vs External

A key distinction of Robbins' model is that:

Resourceful = Internal
Unresourceful = External

The most important thing is to take 100% ownership of our own space and how we meet our needs, rather than to outsource them to our external world. While ever we are dependent on things or people to meet our core needs we are on dangerous ground. The moment one of these things gets threatened or someone doesn't behave how we need them to, our whole sense of happiness and well-being is jeopardised. The person who holds onto their power and does not experience hurtfulness while doing so, is the person who can look themselves in the mirror and say, "I am a good person whether you agree, accept, acknowledge believe in, think I'm doing the right thing—my significance is not up for grabs!"

Children are born with a very high sense of self. If you have any doubt about the truth of this statement, merely observe a toddler who has need of something. They do not hesitate to let their world know that they expect this need to be met. They don't care whether the adults are asleep, eating, talking, watching T.V. or otherwise occupied. The moment the child is tired, hungry, thirsty or bored they cry out for someone to come fix their problem. The challenge with this high sense of self is hanging onto it as you get older and less attention is focused on you.

Imagine being the first born child to adoring parents who are a well-connected part of a loving extended family. You become the centre of attention for this entire family for the first two years of your life. There will be thousands of photos, cuddles, gifts from parents, grandparents, uncles and aunts as well as close friends. The naturally high sense of self you have been born with is completely reflected back to you by your world. It is such a safe and loving environment. Then from nowhere, tragedy strikes... baby number two comes along. All of a sudden there is a shift in the centre of gravity. You are now expected to do stuff on your own. Mum and dad, grandma and grandpa are now focused on the new born. You have become yesterday's news. You are not as cute or clever. Your tricks are boring and common. For the first time in your short life, your high sense of self is no longer being reflected back to you. You are left to question the truth of your own worth. You are left to find new ways to attract attention and affection.[38] It makes sense that this whole experience is incredibly emotionally unstable for the child. Their safe world becomes volatile and they experience uncertainty for the first time.

Paradoxically, their high sense of self-belief and entitlement, which has served them so well, now poses the biggest threat to their emotional and psychological health. To hold onto it and not have it reflected back to them all the time creates a roller coaster ride that, for a child, can become dangerous and traumatic. They do not have the emotional resilience and maturity to cope with these fluctuations and so almost inevitably take the safer option and opt to let go of the high belief. They settle for taking their cues about their value and worth from their external world.

They give up ownership of their own significance, handing the responsibility for meeting this need to others. The child quickly learns that they will get what they need when they perform, please, and meet the expectations of those around them. This is the beginning of a new external strategy for meeting their need, replacing their original internal one. While the new strategy may well be safer for them in this season of life, it very quickly becomes problematic. It leads to all kinds of neediness which leaves them vulnerable to hurtfulness. This in turn causes the child to develop limiting beliefs about their own adequacy. They are left wondering if they are good enough, pretty enough, smart enough or just plain enough.

Dealing with Limiting Beliefs About Self

In order to return to our original, more resourceful strategy for significance it is important to first deal with our limiting beliefs about self. In addition to what we've already covered in chapter 9, here is a four step process for achieving this:

a) Realise you had a high belief from birth
A high sense of self was yours. You had it. You knew without a shadow of a doubt that you were totally valuable, worthwhile and deserving of love the moment you drew breath. Everything was fine while you were getting it reflected back to you, but the moment the consistency of this feedback changed...

b) You let go of it to be safe
Your high sense of self was not taken from you. You are not a victim. YOU did the loving thing and let go of something that was a threat to your emotional health and therefore...

c) You can pick it up again when it is safe
For most people, there will never be a time where it feels safe enough to pick up their high sense of self again. As a result they will live the rest of your life limited by an underlying fear of their own inadequacy. However, in order to make it safe for you to pick it up again you will need to reframe safety and examine what you really need to be afraid of.

d) Reframe safety
What do you really need protecting from? What really is the biggest threat to your happiness and well-being. You are 100% wired for self-preservation and safety. It would be foolish to think you could just turn off your need for safety. Rather you need to refocus your defences onto the most significant threats rather than the most immediate. The people who succeed in life don't have less fear and more courage; they simply fear

different things. To them their biggest fears are around not achieving their potential, wasting their lives or getting to the end of their life realising they have played it safe and stayed small.

I cut my teeth in the coaching world working with the long term unemployed. I developed a six week coaching program totally focused on dealing with the internal barriers of fear, insecurity and limiting beliefs that held people back from meaningful work. I learnt so much about the wonder of how people work dealing with those who were feeling incredibly stuck, facing their mountain of change.

One of my favourite experiences was with a young man at an employment agency. The employment consultants were at their wits end. They had all but given up on him, believing him to be beyond help. They explained that this guy had been on their books for three years and had resisted every attempt they had made to find him work. He seemed to have zero motivation to do anything with his life except sit in a dark room all day playing computer games. His dad was enabling the behaviour by bankrolling him, which further frustrated all attempts to get him to function responsibly in the real world. His employment consultant handed him over to me and wished me luck. I walked into the room where he was seated, closed the door behind myself and sat down across from him.

"G'day mate… I'm Jaemin. I was just wondering… are you a piece of shit?"

I had his attention. He stood up and pointed at me.

"How dare you call me that… Who do you think you are?"

I met his threatening aggression with a huge smile and reached out to shake his hand.

"Fantastic" I said. "I didn't think you were, it's just that I'd been told you were a no hoper who was basically a waste of space. I couldn't believe that was true but I thought I'd check in and find out from you."

It was a high-risk strategy that almost left me with a black eye—and I may never repeat again—but it worked. I had him. He could not play the 'no-hoper' game with me because he just told me he wasn't a worthless piece of shit.

Deep down, we all know that we are incredible, valuable and worthwhile. So why do we invest everything we have into protecting ourselves from the failure, disappointment and judgment? In that moment, this young man had owned his value. He had seen it and so had I. It was the beginning of him turning his life around.

Honour

Another key aspect of 100% ownership is honour.[39] One of the most common and painful occurrences of hurtfulness often happens with our own parents. The first seven years of life are definitely the most impressionable in terms of developing belief systems and values for life. Inevitably, where a person has self-love issues, there has been a lack in the way their parents have nurtured love into their lives in these early years.

The fifth of the Ten Commandments is, "Honour your mother and father that it may go well with you." (Exodus 20:12) The term 'honour' as used in the Ten Commandments means 'to give due weight to' or 'to weigh appropriately'. The origin of the word comes from the marketplace where a seller would have his product at the table, along with a pair of scales. The buyer would come, evaluate the product and weigh it in the scales. The seller would examine the currency and test it for genuineness. Each would weigh the other person's offering and then they would 'honour the agreement' and exchange. To honour your parents actually means that you need to weigh the good and the bad fairly, instead of dismissing the bad and overplaying the good, or forgetting the good and focusing entirely on the bad. When a person dismisses the negative things that their parents did, they reinforce their low self-esteem. Those with low self-esteem will overestimate the weight of another, and under estimate self-value.

When people say that the bad things done to them don't really matter, they are saying that they don't matter and that they don't really deserve to be loved well. The logic is flawed. Justifying the poor behaviour or weakness of your parents due to how they were raised and the lack in the way they were parented themselves doesn't cut it either. Have you ever heard a parent excuse themselves from loving their own children with all they've got simply because their parents weren't good at showing love? It may feel inappropriate to bring up negative things about your parents, but this is not about judging or criticising them. In order to weigh them appropriately, and ultimately forgive them where they failed, you need to own the fact that you deserved better at times. You are a person of inherent value who deserved to be treated as such.

There are times where anger is the appropriate emotional response to the process of honouring your parents. Anger is not by definition a negative emotion. Rather, it is a very powerful and pure emotion designed to cause you to take action that you wouldn't have been prepared to take otherwise. At its core, anger is about recognising that something is unfair or unjust. To weigh the bad is to be angry with evil done to you, to recognise that you deserved better and acknowledge that it is not OK.

It is only when you own your own significance in this way that you are able to forgive. It is impossible to forgive without first giving due weight to the issue. When you say you have forgiven without having properly weighed the situation, all you have really done is swept the issue under the carpet so it is out of sight. It still lurks beneath the surface threatening to rear its ugly head at any moment. There is nothing to forgive if we have justified the issue and said it didn't matter. Forgiveness is not necessarily a decision to trust the person or even be close to them again; instead it is about letting go of your right to hurt them back. In doing so, you free yourself from that person and that event and render it powerless to hurt you any longer. When you are unable to forgive, you actually hold the person and the event close to yourself and give them the power to hurt you again and again.

I encourage you take a moment to truly honour your parents. Write down a list of all the good and bad things they did to you. When your list is complete, read through it out loud and say the things that need saying while being free to feel the associated emotion. It is rarely appropriate or necessary for you to have the honour conversation face to face with your parents, but the injustice needs to be verbalized loud enough for you to hear it with your own ears.

Personal Boundaries

In the power struggle that ensues between those who used to oppress us, and our new sense of self-empowerment, it is going to become important to establish good boundaries. The purpose of a boundary is to protect and differentiate between what is mine and what is yours. A farmer builds fences so that the neighbours are aware of where their land ends and his begins and to protect valuable property and livestock from being mistaken as free for others to use for their own purpose.

We need to be able to tell other people when they are acting in ways that are not acceptable to us. Learning to set boundaries is about discovering that I don't have the power to make you feel a certain way, therefore your feelings are not my fault or responsibility. Likewise, the way I feel is not your fault or responsibility. I establish a boundary, which marks the edge of my property, my paddock. My feelings are in my paddock, so I have the power to control them. They are not in your paddock, so you have no power to control how I feel.

Often people with poor boundaries are overly positive, peacekeepers or selfless people pleasers. They always seem cheerful and generous, but beyond the well-trained cheery veneer they are likely to be feeling jaded, taken advantage of, insecure and weak.

I was talking with someone recently who was explaining with pride their position on an upcoming family gathering. There had been a history of hurt, offence, miscommunications and people being rubbed the wrong way when a certain couple were present. This person had decided that nothing was going to get to them this time. They said they were not going to be ruffled by any behaviour and would cope with any situation that arose. Even though this idea sounded very noble, they were actually operating from a place of poor self-significance and low self-esteem.

To be OK with *any* behaviour is to accept other people's foolishness at your expense. Being a doormat that others walk all over in the name of 'keeping the peace' only undermines your own sense of self and teaches other people that it is OK to treat you that way. There are some things that you should not be OK with, especially when they violate what is sacred within you. If you say it doesn't matter, you say you don't matter. You dishonour yourself and you dishonour the other person.

Once you begin to establish boundaries, internally owning your emotions and externally guarding your boundaries (not putting up with other people's bad behaviour and violations) it is important to have the capacity to maintain these boundaries, standing strong against the bad behaviour which is sure to come. In order to do this, you need to build your own resilience by considering your ongoing relationship with yourself, continuing to invest in your own personal development.

Becoming an Adult

Stephen Covey explains that the journey towards maturity goes from *dependence*, to *independence* to *interdependence*.[40] The example he gives is of a child who begins life totally dependent on its parents for survival, but then as it grows, should become mature enough to eventually leave home and learn to provide for its own needs. From this place of independence, the person can then form meaningful interdependent relationships. They no longer need each other to survive but can contribute meaningfully into the other person's life out of the depth of who they are.

It is natural to start out being dependent upon others to validate us through their acceptance and approval. However, if we never find a way to break free from needing this from others and learn to do it for ourselves, we never really become adults.

The aim of the game is not for you to become completely self-sufficient, isolated and independent, completely internally referenced and needing nobody. But if you don't pass through the stormy seas of independence, you never get to the promised land of interdependent relationships where you are free to give and receive in a way that adds value to you and others.

Questions

- *As you review the six core needs model, what areas strike you as needing work in your own life?*

- *In those areas, can you identify any unresourceful behaviours?*

- *Have you become clear about the intention of these negative behaviours?*

- *What else could you do that meets the original, underlying intention, but is also aligned to your values?*

- *Where are you at the moment on the journey towards maturity? Are you dependent, independent or interdependent?*

Chapter Eighteen

HUMOUR

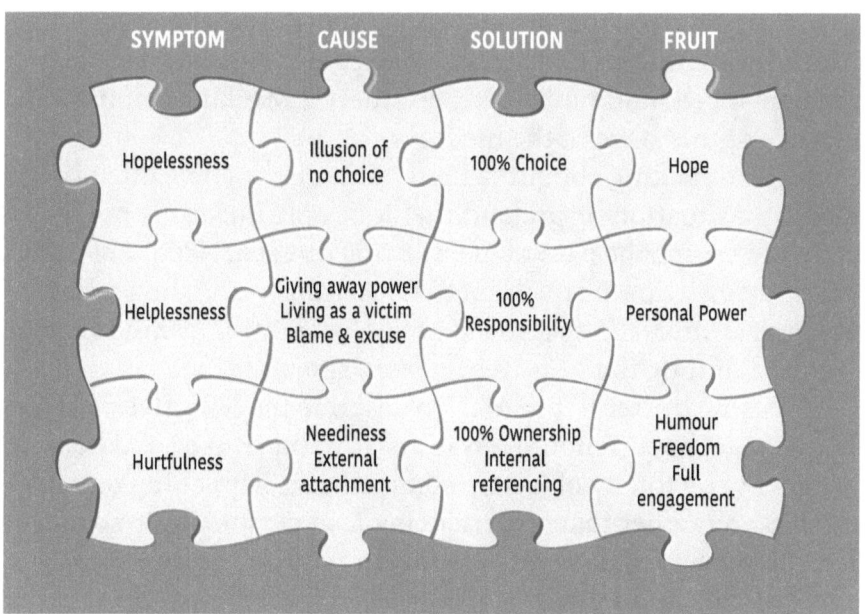

You know you have escaped hurtfulness when you are free of what used to be hurtful. Indeed it is now almost funny. You are able to be totally objective about the situation rather than experiencing it so personally.

Fruit 3: Humour

It is common for people to imagine they are free from the hurtfulness in their life when in fact they have just found a way to avoid the people or situations that have historically caused them grief. The moment they are back in contact with the bullies or villains again, they experience strong emotional responses just like old times.

When we have really embraced 100% ownership of our value and worth and have internally referenced our success and significance we find ourselves experiencing life in a way that was previously unavailable to us. I use the word 'humour' to describe the sense of freedom and lightness that flows when we escape hurtfulness. You might find this choice of language strange, but I'm convinced humour is such a wonderful word that captures the essence of this stage in the model.

I am not talking about the kind of humour people often use to dismiss a situation or pretend that it doesn't hurt. It is not about trying to escape the pain of life by being sarcastic, laughing things off or saying it doesn't really matter. It certainly isn't about learning to laugh at yourself. It's also not about just putting a smile on your face and finding the positives in every situation.

I'm using the term 'humour' to describe the objectivity you get by no longer being emotionally invested in the situation. When you are able to be totally objective about what is happening to you or around you rather than experiencing it so personally, it no longer has the power to hurt you. When you remove the neediness you are then able to see other people's behaviour for what it really is. If they are carrying on like a pork chop, that becomes their problem not yours. Tantrums, game playing, manipulation, bullying, and the like all lose their power to affect you. It's crazy that what once caused you so much grief is not even touching you. There is a liberty, a freedom and joy that comes from not having the old, strong emotional response. In fact, you almost have no emotional response at all.

Think again of the disempowered housewife. Imagine you were a fly on the wall listening to the conversations taking place after she took 100% responsibility and got her personal power back. She's trying to retrain her husband. Do you imagine you'd be hearing high-quality, caring and respectful talk from him? Of course not... there would be game playing, accusations and obfuscation. The conversation would be highly emotional, circular and childish. If you were to listen without being enmeshed in the situation, I'm sure you would be astounded at what you were hearing. You would probably be thinking, 'Hang on a minute, you said what? And then you backed down? How old are you people? This is crazy. In fact, this is so crazy it is funny!'

Humour is the natural response when you can see madness for what it is without being emotionally invested in it in any way, shape or form. The conversation between the husband and wife is anything but funny to them because they're emotionally invested in the situation. For them it's incredibly frustrating, unfair and hurtful. With a different frame though, it can be experienced totally differently.

When you break free from the situation and are no longer needy or attached, you are able to see it for what it is... often for the first time. The overriding sense could be one of amazement: 'Wow! What used to be so upsetting and hurtful now isn't even touching me! Isn't that funny? Now I can see that once powerful person as an insecure child. Wow! Isn't that funny?'

When we are watching a film or reading a book, certain plot twists can become very exciting, and very powerful. One of the most used is the dethroning of the oppressor, or the exposing of the villain. Up until the point of dethronement there has been tension building and trouble brewing, but when the plot twists you experience great relief, which can even be funny.

The Svengali[41] (one who exerts excessive control or manipulation) loses his or her power. You finally see them for the scared little child they really are.

Letting go of the can

Humour proves that you are really free. It's the freedom that comes when you are finally able to let go of the things that are causing the most pain. So often we feel that the things that are causing us the most grief in life are holding onto us, when really we are holding onto them.

My favourite example of this comes from 'The Simpsons'[42] Walking home from work one day, Homer ends up getting both hands stuck inside vending machines while trying to steal their contents. In the next scene we see the area all cordoned off. The fire brigade and emergency services are there attempting to rescue Homer from this awful predicament.

Fireman: "Mr Simpson, there is no easy way to say this, we're going to have to saw your arms off."

Homer: "Awww, but they'll grow back won't they?"

Fireman: "Yeah sure… they'll grow back."

Other Fireman: "Ah…Homer, are you just holding onto the can?"

Homer: "Yeah… why?"

Letting Go of the Can

Change may take a long time coming, but it can happen in a moment. As unbelievable as it may sound, you can have change as soon as you really want it. You don't have to work hard for it. Once you decide to let go of the can, situations that once seemed so hopeless and caused you to feel helpless and hurt, now seem so simple and easy to escape from. When you do that, there is a lightness and freedom that comes as fruit of taking 100% ownership for your own value and worth rather than contracting it out to your external world.

How funny it is that all along you were choosing to remain in the situation because of what you needed from it. When the neediness is gone, you are totally capable of walking free.

Added Bonus... Eliminating Obligation, Expectations and Others' Foolishness

When a person experiences the stage of humour and freedom as fruit of taking 100% ownership, obligation (doing things you don't want to do but feel you have to do), expectation (living according to other peoples rules and expectations of what you should or shouldn't be doing) and tolerating others foolishness (putting up with being used and abused) almost magically drop out of their lives as well. These three things are the source of so much pain and anger. When there is nothing to prove or earn and you are truly free, these three things quickly vanish from your life. Let's look at how this works.

Obligation—why would you do something you don't want to do? You don't 'have' to do anything. Everything you do is from a place of 100% choice, and responsibility.

Expectation—why would you live by someone else's rules? That's crazy talk! You don't need their approval or affection or attention. It is your life and you are now taking 100% responsibility for your own results and owning your value and worth completely irrespective of what others say or think about you. I am not suggesting that you stop considering others and only think of your own needs. Rather, I am suggesting that as you take responsibility for your own results you become free to make choices that match your own values and expectations rather than operating in response to other people's expectations.

Others' foolishness—why would you not confront someone who is treating you foolishly? Are you going to fear them or worry about offending them, when they are offending you? You are a person of immense value and worth and it is not OK for people to treat you in any other way. You let go of blame and excuse and realise it is 100% your responsibility to train others how to treat you. I can honestly say there is no one in my world that treats me poorly and there is absolutely nothing I do motivated by a sense of obligation. This certainly wasn't always the case in my life, but it is definitely one of the most enjoyable aspects of applying this model and seeing the fruit come to bear.

When you experience this level of 'humour' you have the ability to dissociate and become objective about what is happening around you, instead of taking everything so personally. It then becomes possible to become assertive and reclaim the ability to say yes and no. I'm convinced that assertiveness is much more of a fruit than a learned skill. It just can't work to strive and learn how to stand up for yourself without having first addressed this issue of hurtfulness. That is a typical behaviour management approach which would inevitably be undermined by any sense of neediness you still carry.

Another amazing fruit of taking 100% ownership is our capacity for full engagement. The person who makes the best parent, spouse, boss, business owner, employee, friend etc. is the person who doesn't need to be any of those things. They are there only because they have chosen to be. There is nothing to prove and nothing to earn. They are not attached to their role and they are not defined by it. They are able to finally be fully present and unguarded. They are able to bring their best.

That is such a healthy place from which to create amazing relationships.

WRAPPING IT ALL UP

All challenges issues or problems we face in life are an example of some form of hopelessness, helplessness or hurtfulness. We experience these symptoms because we are under the illusion that there is no choice, because we have given away our power or because we have external attachments to success and significance.

While the solutions may not be easy, they are always elegantly simple. Too often people confuse simple with easy. The truth is, it will be simple and hard. Embracing 100% choice, taking 100% responsibility and recognising 100% ownership—as we develop internal reference for our value and significance—is never easy. It is the deepest and most important work of our life. And just because we did well at it yesterday, is no guarantee that we will nail it today or tomorrow.

Remember that if you don't know what you want in life, you will end up serving the agenda of those who do. The moment you lose sight of your desires and dreams, taking the road less travelled always seems too hard. Having a compelling vision for your life is the only thing powerful enough to cause you to keep dealing with all your stuff. You will only choose the harder road when you realise that no other road will lead you to see your dreams fulfilled and the longings of your heart satisfied.

I encourage you to keep firmly focused on exactly what you would like to achieve in this life. You must know what you want every day that you get out of bed and your feet hit the ground. Remember that if you don't know what you want in life, you will end up serving the agenda of those who do. The moment you lose sight of your desires and dreams, taking the road less travelled always seems too hard. You will only choose the harder road when you realise that no other road will lead you to see your dreams fulfilled and the longings of your heart satisfied.

May you find companions for your journey and be a companion for others on theirs…

ENDNOTES

Preface

1. A reference to the classic book written by M. Scott Peck – The road less travelled. Penguin Books
2. Henry David Thoreau, (1817–62) Walden, chapter 1, p. 8 (1966). Originally published in 1854.
3. This quote is paraphrased from Tolle, E. 2005: A new earth. London: Penguin Books, pp11-12.
4. Again, I have paraphrased the teaching of Eckhart Tolle. "A new earth" Page 13.

Chapter Two

5. The SMART acronym first appeared in the November 1981 issue of Management Review. "There's a S.M.A.R.T. way to write management goals and objectives." was the title and it was written by George Doran, Arthur Miller, and James Cunningham. I'm not sure who first added the ER on the end to make it SMARTER, but these two extra words add a lot to the model.

Chapter Three

6   Tolle, E. 2005 (as n.3 above) p134.
7   Robbins, A. 2003: *Awaken the Giant Within*. New York: Free Press, p47.
8   Covey, S. 1989: *7 Habits of Highly Effective People*. Melbourne: The Business Library, p66.
9   The idea of internal signalling and rapport with self comes from John Grinder. This is a radically different approach to the typical labelling of internal issues as sickness, and conditions. Dr Ian Snape has added work around creating contracts with self between the conscious and unconscious to maintain trust and the ability to be aligned in working toward the same outcome.
10 Brand, P. 1993: *The gift of pain. Grand Rapids*: Zondervan, pp4-5.
11 Brand, P. 1993 (as n.10 above)
12 Dr. Ian Snape from 'The Coaching Space' in Hobart introduced me to this question for building rapport with self. www.thecoachingspace.com.au
13 The notion of irrational fear is further explored in this article: http://www.theatlantic.com/health/archive/2014/10/the-psychology-of-irrational-fear/382080/
14 O'Conner, J. 2001: The NLP Workbook: *A Practical Guide to Achieving the Results You Want*. London: Element, NLP Presupposition Nine
15 This comes from the idea that all behaviour has a positive intention. O'Connor, J. 2001 (as n.14 above)
16 Scott, S. 2002: *Fierce Conversations*. New York: Berkley books, p77.
17 This exercise is called adopting perceptual positions and was created by John Grinder in 1990.

Chapter Four

18 O'Connor, J. 2001 (as n.14 above), NLP presupposition No. 4.
19 Bandler, R., Grinder, R. and Andreas, S. 1979: Frogs into Princes: Neuro Linguistic Programming. Moab, Utah: Real People Press.
20 The term secondary gain was made famous by Dr. Phil McGraw, but it was first published as a term to describe patients that gained an advantage by being sick in the following article: Davidhizar, R. 1994: The pursuit of illness for secondary gain. Health Care Supervisor, 13:1, p10-5.
21 This is basically the Six Step Reframe Process as outlined in O'Connor, J. 2001 (as n.10 above), pp234-7.

Chapter Five

22 Tolle, E. 2005 (as n.3 above), p15
23 Richard Bandler and John Grinder developed the concept of 'Delete, Distort and Generalise' in their Internal Representation (I/R) model of communication.
24 Keller, H. 1946: *Let Us Have Faith*, Garden City, New York: Doubleday & Company, pp50, 51.
25 Stearns, M. 2004: *Conscious Courage: Turning Everyday Challenges Into Opportunities*. Seminole, Florida: Enrichment Books, p15.
26 Questions 11-14: Dorsey, J. "Reframe Problems" at *http://www.success.com*

Chapter Six

27 "You can learn NLP techniques for controlling your state of mind and in this way you can control your outcome." Adler, H. 2002: *Handbook of NLP: A Manual for Professional Communicators*, Gower Publishing Company, pp54-55.
28 Bandler et al. 1979 (as n.19 above)
29 Anthony Robbins was the first to identify that we can master our emotional states with a specific recipe of how we use our body, focus, and language. *http://training.tonyrobbins.com/master-your-emotional-health-and-master-your-life/*
30 The Be Do Have model is one of my favourite coaching tools. Both Stephen Covey and Anthony Robbins use it in their writing, yet I believe it predates both of them.
31 Helmstetter, S. 1991: *What to Say When You are Talking to Yourself*. London: Thorsons, p18.
32 Dilts, R. "Anchoring". http://www.nlpu.com/Articles/artic28.htm

Chapter Seven

33 Stankavich, M. 2014: What is the correlation between happiness and one's career choices? *http://www.ted.com/conversations/23941/what_is_the_correlation_betwee_1.html*

Chapter Nine

34 Covey, S. 1989 (as n.8 above) p69.
35 The NLP communication Model was developed by John Ginder and Richard Bandler as the basis of how we communicate to ourselves and others.

Chapter Sixteen

36 Tolle, E. 2005 (as n.3 above) p76

Chapter Seventeen

37 Robbins, A. 2000: *Get the Edge 10 Day Audio Series, Disc 2*. San Diego: Robbins Research International Inc.
38 Leman, K. 2009: *The Birth Order Book*. Grand Rapids: Revel, Chapter 2.
39 I first heard honour explained like this by Ps. Alan Meyer of Care Force Church.
40 Covey, S. 1989 (as n.8 above) p49

Chapter Eighteen

41 Svengali is a fictional character in George du Maurier's 1895 novel 'Trilby'.
42 The Simpsons, Created by Matt Groening. Season 5, Episode 6

www.ingramcontent.com/pod-product-compliance
Lightning Source LLC
Chambersburg PA
CBHW020613300426
44113CB00007B/625